NCIDQ® INTERIOR DESIGN PRACTICUM

PRACTICE EXAM

DAVID KENT BALLAST, FAIA
NCIDQ® CERTIFICATE NO. 9425

The Power to Pass™
www.ppi2pass.com

Professional Publications, Inc. • Belmont, California

NCIDQ® is a registered trademark of the National Council for Interior Design Qualification.

PPI is not affiliated with the National Council for Interior Design Qualification (NCIDQ®). PPI does not administer the NCIDQ Exam. PPI does not claim any endorsement or recommendation of its products or services by NCIDQ.

NCIDQ® Interior Design Practicum Practice Exam

Current printing of this edition: 1

Printing History

edition number	printing number	update
1	1	New book.

Cover design by Amy Schwertman La Russa.

Printed in the United States of America.

PPI
1250 Fifth Avenue, Belmont, CA 94002
(650) 593-9119
www.ppi2pass.com

ISBN: 978-1-59126-425-5

TABLE OF CONTENTS

PART B SOLUTIONS

PART C SOLUTIONS

PREFACE AND ACKNOWLEDGMENTS

Every five years, the National Council for Interior Design Qualification (NCIDQ)[1] commissions a practice analysis to ensure the exam continues to accurately assess the knowledge and skills interior designers need to practice responsibly and to protect the health, safety, and welfare of the public. Results of the practice analysis are reported in the council's publication *Analysis of the Interior Design Profession*. The council administers three exams (the Interior Design Fundamentals Exam (IDFX), the Interior Design Professional Exam (IDPX), and the Interior Design Practicum) that cover the content areas identified in the analysis as being the essential tasks, knowledge, and skills of interior designers in the United States and Canada. I wrote *NCIDQ Interior Design Practicum Practice Exam* to be consistent with the Practicum's content areas so that you will use it to prepare for and pass the Practicum.

Many people have helped in the production of this book. I would like to thank Sarah Hubbard, director of product development and implementation; Cathy Schrott, production services manager; Christine Eng, product development manager; Chelsea Logan and Julia White, editorial project managers; Magnolia Molcan, copy editor; and Kate Hayes, production associate.

While I had a lot of help with this book, any mistakes are mine alone. If you find a mistake, please submit it through PPI's error reporting system at **www.ppi2pass.com/errata**. A reply will be posted and the error revised accordingly in the next printing.

David Kent Ballast, FAIA
NCIDQ® Certificate No. 9425

---

[1]In this Preface, I refer to the National Council for Interior Design Qualification as "the council," and the National Council for Interior Design Qualification exam as "the exam."

INTRODUCTION

HOW TO USE THIS BOOK

NCIDQ Interior Design Practicum Practice Exam was developed in accordance with the National Council for Interior Design Qualification (NCIDQ)[1] Practicum content areas. Though the exact exercises in this book won't be found on the actual exam, they are like Practicum exercises in terms of their format, level of difficulty, and the content areas they cover.

The seven exercises in this book are organized according to the three parts of the Practicum, as given in Table 1 in this Introduction. Each exercise includes a project description, a list of project requirements, and a set of design instructions. The solution for each exercise should be drawn on the appropriate worksheet. The worksheets presented in this book have been scaled for ease of publication and are accurately drawn at the scales indicated on each sheet. You may work the exercises by photocopying the scaled worksheets, filling them out according to the instructions and requirements, and comparing your solutions to those provided in this book. Alternatively, you may work the exercises with realistic, exam-sized layouts and scales. 18″ × 24″ PDF images of the worksheets may be downloaded at **www.ppi2pass.com/ idpcpxdrawings**. Without access to a large-format printer, you may need to assemble worksheet pages from multiple smaller sheets. Instructions for how to print the worksheets using standard printers are provided at the download link.

Use the *Interior Design Reference Manual: Everything You Need to Know to Pass the NCIDQ Exam* (IDRM, also published by PPI) to research less familiar topics. Taking the time to research less familiar topics will help you strengthen your understanding and ensure exam readiness. Also review this book's "Exercise Building Code Requirements" section. Solutions to the seven practice exam exercises must comply with the code requirements in it.

---

[1]The National Council for Interior Design Qualification is referred to as "the council" throughout this Introduction, while the National Council for Interior Design Qualification exam is referred to as "the exam."

Once you are comfortable with the range of material covered, set aside a full day—eight hours plus a lunch break—to work all seven exercises in this book. Put away study materials and references, set a timer, and use the drawing sheets to complete the exercises as best as you can within the time limit. (Table 1 in this Introduction gives the time limits for each part of the exam, and each exercise in this book gives a target time for completing the solution.) Mimic the actual exam experience in every way possible.

If time allows, review your work. If time runs out before you are able to complete all the exercises, make a note of the last exercise you worked within the time limit, but continue on to complete the entire practice exam. Keep track of time to determine how much faster you would need to work to finish the actual exam within eight hours.

After completing the practice exam, check your solutions against the sample passing and failing solutions in the back of this book. Solutions illustrate ways of completing the exercises satisfactorily, as well as common errors and oversights. For some exercises, a number of different approaches resulting in a passing solution will be possible. If your solution satisfies all the program requirements while avoiding major mistakes, it will be satisfactory even if it is different from the passing solution given in this book.

ABOUT THE NCIDQ EXAM

The exam is divided into three sections: the Interior Design Fundamentals Exam (IDFX), the Interior Design Professional Exam (IDPX), and the Interior Design Practicum. IDFX and IDPX are taken on a computer, while the Practicum is taken on paper. IDFX contains questions testing knowledge gained in school (e.g., programming, design application, building systems, construction document standards, drawing standards, and design communication). IDPX contains questions testing knowledge gained through work experience (e.g., codes, building systems, specifications, construction document standards, contract administration, project coordination, and professional practice). There is some content area overlap between IDFX and IDPX. See "Eligibility" later in this Introduction for information on requirements for each exam. IDFX and IDPX are given over a nine-day window in spring and fall. The Practicum is administered twice a year in April and October.

IDFX and IDPX include text- and illustration-based multiple-choice questions. Each question includes four answer options. For example, a question may ask "Where is information about electrical outlets for portable lamps most likely to be found?" and the options given may be

 (A) furniture plan

 (B) partition plan

 (C) power plan

 (D) reflected ceiling plan

You would choose the best answer among the four options by clicking on the appropriate choice. (In the example given, you would choose answer option C.) Both IDFX and IDPX are machine graded.

The Practicum includes individual exercises that will require you to interpret a program, translate it into schematics, produce plan drawings, and develop appropriate specifications and schedules. Refer to "Scoring Method" later in this Introduction for information on how the Practicum is graded.

IDFX is three hours long with 125 questions (100 of which are scored), and IDPX is four hours long with 175 questions (150 of which are scored). The remaining 25 questions in each are used for developmental purposes and are not scored. (These questions are not identified in advance.) The Practicum is eight hours long and includes seven graded exercises.

ABOUT THE PRACTICUM

The seven Practicum exercises are organized into three parts, as given in Table 1. Each part's time allowance and the percentage of weight given to each exercise are also given in Table 1.

Table 1 Practicum Exercises

part	exercise	time allowance	
Part A		4 hrs	
	Space Planning		23%
	Lighting Design		11%
Part B		2 hrs	
	Egress		18%
	Life Safety		18%
	Restroom (Washroom)		9%
Part C		2 hrs	
	Systems Integration		12%
	Millwork		9%

The exam requires familiarity with universal design principles, as well as with the code requirements in the *NCIDQ Building Code Requirements* document at www.ncidq.org. Review this document well before the exam date. Exam exercises will be graded in accordance with these requirements.

The Seven Practicum Exercises

Each of the Space Planning, Lighting Design, Egress, and Millwork exercises is based on either a commercial or a residential building type. The Life Safety, Restroom (Washroom), and Systems Integration exercises are generally based on commercial uses. The following descriptions outline the basic requirements for adequately solving the exercises. Unless otherwise noted, all references to scale in this section refer to scales typical for the NCIDQ exam. (This book uses worksheets that have been scaled for ease of publication.) The recommended solving times are provided for guidance only. On the actual exam, more or less time may be spent on an exercise than what is noted here.

Exercise 1: Space Planning
Recommended time: **3 hours**

You are given project requirements for a space with an area between 2200 ft² and 2600 ft² (204.4 m² and 241.5 m²). The requirements include between 15 and 20 individual spaces, their furnishings, and their basic adjacency requirements. Plumbing must be located within a certain distance of water supply and drains. Other factors must also be accommodated, possibly including existing mechanical or electrical services and the locations of doors, windows, and other fixed items. The Space Planning exercise is drawn at $^{1}/_{4}$ in (1:50) scale.

You must sketch a floor plan with the required spaces and adjacencies and locate a second means of egress. Each space must be labeled with its name and area. All furnishings listed in the project requirements must be drawn and the power/voice/data outlets for three or four designated spaces must be indicated using the symbol legend provided. Barrier-free clearances in changes of direction, at doorways, and at plumbing fixtures must be correctly provided. All other code requirements given in the exam booklet must also be satisfied.

Exercise 2: Lighting Design

***Recommended time:* 1 hour**

You are given the floor plan and reflected ceiling plan for a small space with an area between 550 ft² and 850 ft² (51.1 m² and 78.9 m²), along with abbreviated cut sheets for 16 different luminaires. Plans for the Lighting Design exercise are drawn at $^{1}/_{4}$ in (1:50) scale. Using only the luminaires listed, select the appropriate types to satisfy the exercise's lighting criteria in such a way that the total energy use limit, given in watts per square foot (square meter), is not exceeded.

You must draw the lighting plan on the reflected ceiling plan using the symbols for the luminaires as given on the cut sheets. Switching must be indicated using the symbols from the switching legend given on the plan. In one area, the location of the luminaires must be dimensioned. If wall sconces are used, their mounting heights must be indicated.

You must also complete a lighting schedule, showing the types of luminaires used, how many of each type, and the rationale for selecting each type. Calculate total wattage and divide it by the total area to determine the number of watts per square foot (square meter).

Exercise 3: Egress
***Recommended time:* 1 hour**

You are given the floor plan of a space with an area between approximately 10,000 ft² and 13,500 ft² (929 m² and 1254.2 m²). The floor plan is drawn at $^{1}/_{8}$ in (1:100) scale. The core of the building, which is given, includes two means of egress, typically stairways. A tenant already occupies part of the space, and space planning has been completed for the tenant space and is shown on the plan. You are also given a list of four additional spaces that are needed, with their required occupancies and areas.

To complete this exercise, you must subdivide the rest of the floor to provide for these four additional spaces, and label each space with its area and occupancy load. Plan and show demising walls and egress doors leading to the public corridor. If two exits are required for a space (and they will be for at least one), you must determine both door locations and correctly dimension the distance between them to satisfy the code requirements.

For the existing tenant space, you must draw and dimension the common path of travel and the travel distance to the exit stairs. Calculate the occupant load for each exit stair and write both loads on the drawing in the area labeled for "notes." Barrier-free clearances must be shown at changes in direction along all egress routes.

Exercise 4: Life Safety

Recommended time: **30 minutes**

You are given a floor plan with furnishings for a commercial tenant space with an area between approximately 3000 ft² and 5000 ft² (278.7 m² and 464.5 m²). The floor plan is drawn at ¹/₈ in (1:100) scale. Drawings of door types, frame types and legends of abbreviations and symbols to use in the schedules and on the plan are also provided. Brief project requirements for hardware, security, acoustic privacy, and other factors, as well as building code requirements relevant to life safety are included.

On the plan, certain partitions and doors are labeled. To complete the exercise, you must determine where to place smoke detectors, fire extinguishers, audio/visual fire alarms, exit signs, and emergency lighting in the space. For each labeled partition, use the partition schedule to indicate fire rating, height, and whether the partition must be acoustical. For each labeled door, use the door/frame/hardware schedule to indicate height, door type and material, frame type and material, and hardware type.

Exercise 5: Restroom (Washroom)
Recommended time: **30 minutes**

You are given an empty floor plan of a space with an area between 200 ft² and 250 ft² (18.6 m² and 23.2 m²). The floor plan is drawn at ¹/₄ in (1:50) scale. Using requirements given in the problem statement and in the accessibility codes, lay out the fixtures and equipment for a men's restroom. Two toilet stalls, two urinals, and two lavatories must be placed, and locations must be determined for grab bars, mirrors, soap dispensers, and other washroom accessories. You must also choose the substrate and finish for the wet wall.

The fixtures must be dimensioned and consideration must be given to sight lines. The mounting height of each accessory must be indicated on a fixture and accessory schedule.

Exercise 6: Systems Integration
Recommended time: **1 hour**

You are given two sheets of drawings. One sheet contains a reflected ceiling and furniture plan of a space with an area between 1500 ft² and 5000 ft² (139.4 m² and 464.5 m²), along with a completed lighting schedule and a blank table in which to make notes for the mechanical, plumbing, and electrical contractors. On the reflected ceiling plan are eight cloud notations with corresponding numbers. Each cloud indicates the location of a coordination conflict among the structural, mechanical, electrical, sprinkler, and furniture layouts. The other sheet contains a mechanical and sprinkler plan for the same space, details of two types of ceilings used, and a section showing the exterior wall, window height, and other building information. Plans are drawn at ¹/₈ in (1:100) scale. You must determine what the conflict is at each cloud, and in the blank table write suggestions for resolving the conflict.

The project requirements will indicate what items you can and cannot modify. If your suggestion is to relocate an item, you must draw its new location on the reflected ceiling plan. You will need to draw a suitable location on the plan for an access panel in the ceiling and specify on the lighting schedule an appropriate depth and mounting height for wall sconces.

Exercise 7: Millwork
Recommended time: **1 hour**

You are given a floor plan for either a residential or a commercial project of relatively small area, between approximately 250 ft² and 300 ft² (23.2 m² and 27.9 m²). A short list of project requirements, including designing for accessibility and coordinating with existing plumbing is also provided.

You must draw a plan of the millwork at $^1/_4$ in (1:50) scale, as well as one elevation and one section at $^3/_4$ in (1:20) scale to indicate constructability; clearances for accessibility; coordination with plumbing, electrical, and mechanical contractors; and the substrates and finishes of the millwork.

Scoring Method

Solutions to the Practicum are evaluated by qualified NCIDQ graders using a standard and well-defined set of scoring criteria, though professional judgment may also be used. Each exercise is reviewed by two independent graders who look at the entire solution.

Each grader gives a numerical score ranging from zero to five, as shown in Table 2. The score for each exercise indicates the extent to which you've demonstrated competence in solving the exercise. Note that your solution does not have to be perfect to pass, or even to receive full credit. A few minor mistakes will not fail your solution if you show overall that you possess the knowledge and the skill required to accommodate the users of the space.

Table 2 Exercise Score Ratings*

score	description
0	completely blank solution: given when you've made no attempt to solve the exercise
1	fail or incomplete: given when you've demonstrated few, if any, of the exercise's required skills
2	borderline fail: given when you've submitted a complete solution to the exercise, but you have not demonstrated the required level of knowledge and skill
4	borderline pass: given when you've submitted a complete solution to the exercise, and you have demonstrated the required knowledge and skill, even if you did not meet all of the exercise's required criteria
5	pass: given when you've submitted a complete solution to the exercise, and you have demonstrated the required knowledge and skill, even if you did not meet a few of the less critical required criteria

*Note: The passing scores are 4 and 5 (there is no "3").

If one grader passes the exercise and the other fails it, that exercise will be given a third review by another grader. The two agreeing (passing or failing) scores are used and the remaining score is discarded. The two agreeing scores may not be the same number, but they will both be passing or both be failing.

After each exercise is scored, the two numerical scores are added together. This sum is then multiplied by a weighting factor that represents the relative importance of the skills tested in that exercise. The weighting factor for each exercise is given as a percentage in Table 1.

Practicum Content Areas

The council uses its *Analysis of the Interior Design Profession* to develop the exam content areas, which cover the knowledge and skills that interior designers must possess to protect public health, safety, and welfare. The content areas for the Practicum are as follows. The percentage of weight for each content area is given in parentheses.

1. **Knowledge of and skills in developing a design concept (10%):**

   - programming

   - design theory

2. **Knowledge of and skills in design communication methods and techniques (15%):**

   - written design communication methods and techniques

   - visual design communication methods and techniques

3. **Knowledge of and skills in measuring, drafting, and technical drawing conventions (30%):**

   - construction drawings and schedules

   - architectural woodwork

   - specifications

   - lighting

4. **Knowledge of and skills in analyzing and synthesizing the programmatic information (30%):**

   - theories about the relationship between human behavior and the designed environment

   - building construction

   - sustainable design practices

   - building systems

   - interior finishes and materials

5. **Knowledge of and skills in space planning (15%):**

   - code requirements, laws, standards, and regulations

   - site analysis procedures

   - furniture, fixtures, and equipment (including window treatments and textiles)

HOW TO REGISTER FOR THE EXAM

Registering for the exam is a multi-step process. First you must meet the exam's eligibility requirements, then submit an application and have it accepted. Confirm your eligibility, and begin the application process well before the exam date.

Eligibility

You may take IDFX after you have met the minimum education requirements. You may meet the education requirements by receiving a bachelor of arts or master of fine arts degree from an interior design program accredited by the Council for Interior Design Accreditation (CIDA); a bachelor of arts degree or higher from an interior design program *not* accredited by CIDA with at least 60 semester (or 90 quarter) credits in interior design coursework; a bachelor of arts degree or higher in another major with at least 60 semester (or 90 quarter) credits of interior design coursework that led to a diploma, degree, or certificate; an associate of arts degree with at least 40 semester (or 60 quarter) units in interior design; or a bachelor of arts or master of fine arts degree from an architecture program accredited by the National Architectural Accrediting Board (NAAB) or Canadian Architectural Certification Board (CACB).

You may take IDPX and the Practicum after you have met the education and work experience requirements given in this section. Work experience for which academic credit was received will not count toward the hours required. Passing IDFX is not a prerequisite to taking IDPX and the Practicum, although you must receive a passing score on all three exam sections to earn the NCIDQ certificate.

To be eligible for IDPX and the Practicum with a bachelor of arts or master of fine arts degree from an interior design program accredited by CIDA, you must complete 3520 hours of work experience.[3] At least 1760 of those hours must be accrued after you have met your education requirements.

To be eligible for IDPX and the Practicum with a bachelor of arts degree or higher from an interior design program that is *not* accredited by CIDA, you must complete 3520 hours of work experience. At least 1760 of those hours must be accrued after you have met your education requirements. In addition, at least 60 semester (or 90 quarter) credits must be in interior design coursework.

To be eligible for IDPX and the Practicum with a bachelor of arts degree or higher in another major, you must complete 3520 hours of work experience. At least 1760 of those hours must be accrued after you have met your education requirements. In addition, at least 60 semester (or 90 quarter) credits of interior design coursework must be completed and must have resulted in a diploma, degree, or certificate.

To be eligible for IDPX and the Practicum with an associate of arts degree of 60 semester (or 90 quarter) units in interior design, you must complete 5280 hours of work experience. All these hours must be accrued after you have met your education requirements.

To be eligible for IDPX and the Practicum with an associate of arts degree of 40 semester (or 60 quarter) units in interior design, you must complete 7040 hours of work experience must be competed. All these hours must be accrued after you have met your education requirements.

---

[3]Hours worked under an NCIDQ certificate holder, a licensed/registered interior designer, or an architect who offers interior design services count as "qualified" work experience, and accrue at 100%. Hours worked in alternative situations accrue at lower rates. Hours worked under direct supervision by an interior designer who is not registered, licensed, or an NCIDQ certificate holder accrue at a rate of 75%; work sponsored, but not directly supervised, by the same individual accrues at a rate of 25%. Work hours not supervised by a designer (i.e., supervised by someone other than a designer, or not supervised at all in the case of self-employment) accrue at a rate of 25%. The Interior Design Experience Program (IDEP) offered by the council satisfies your work experience requirement.

To be eligible for IDPX and the Practicum with a bachelor of arts or master of fine arts degree from an architecture program accredited by NAAB or CACB, you must complete 5280 hours of work experience. All these hours must be accrued after you have met your education requirements.

Applying

Exam dates and application deadlines are listed on PPI's website at **www.ppi2pass.com/NCIDQfaq**. The first step in the application process is submitting the online application form and application fee through MyNCIDQ, a section of NCIDQ's website (www.ncidq.org). For IDFX, gather the following supporting materials and mail them to the council in a single package.

- *Candidate authorization and consent form:* This form attests to the truthfulness of the application documents and grants the council permission to evaluate the application. Download and print the form through the council's website. The signed hard copy must be included in your package of supporting materials.

- *Official transcripts:* Download the transcript request form from the council's website and submit it to the registrar (along with any fees the registrar requires) for each college or university you attended. The registrar will return the transcript to you in a sealed envelope which must be included, *unopened*, in your package of supporting materials.

For IDPX and the Practicum, also include the following items in the package.

- *Letters of reference:* Ask three references (employers, clients, or professional peers, not friends or family members) to complete the letter of reference form (available on the council's website). Each reference must put the letter in a sealed envelope with his or her signature across the flap and return it to you. The *unopened* letters must be included in your package of supporting materials.

- *Work experience verification forms:* Submit a separate form for each position you held. Complete the direct supervision work experience verification form for work experience you completed under a direct supervisor. For work experience not directly supervised by a design professional (for example, in the case of self-employment), complete the sponsored work experience verification form. A sponsor is a design professional who can verify work experience, but was not a direct supervisor and may not have had direct control over or detailed knowledge of your work.

Do not include any additional materials in your package of supporting materials. Any additional documents you include will be discarded. Be sure to have all materials submitted by the relevant deadline; the council will not review a partial application, or an application once the deadline has passed.

Registering

If your application is accepted by the council, you will be notified through MyNCIDQ. If your application is not accepted, you may need further education and experience to fulfill the requirements. If this process takes more than one year, you will need to resubmit your entire application.

If your application is accepted, you may register for as many exam sections as you were accepted for. If you choose not to register for this exam cycle, you will remain an active candidate and will receive email notifications about registering for the next exam cycle. Fees are listed in the registration guide (a brochure available for download from the council's website) for each exam section.

Registering Through Prometric

To register for IDFX or IDPX, go to Prometric's website (www.prometric.com/NCIDQ) or call the toll-free number. Choose the exam location and date from those available. All locations accept registrations up to a day before the exam; some locations accept same-day registration. Registration fees are payable by credit card only.

Prometric will send you an email with your registration confirmation and test center information. Bring two forms of identification with you on examination day. One of these must be a government-issued photo ID.

Registering Through MyNCIDQ

To register for the Practicum, go to MyNCIDQ and click on "Exam Registration." Complete the confidentiality agreement and statement of responsibility. Registration fees are payable online by credit card or through the mail by check (this must be received in time for processing).

The council will send you an email with further exam information after receipt of payment and an email with your letter of admission at least two weeks prior to the exam. Print the letter of admission and present it with a government-issued photo ID on examination day.

WHAT TO BRING TO THE EXAM

Reference materials are not allowed for the Practicum. However, you may bring the following items.

• portable drafting board (no smaller than 24 in × 36 in (610 mm × 914 mm)) with a parallel bar. The exam site may or may not have drafting boards. If it does, the drafting boards will be laid flat with the parallel bars (if any) taped down. This is to assure that all test sites offer the same conditions. Whatever drawing surface you bring into the test site must fit within a 30 in × 48 in (762 mm × 1220 mm) area.

Although all sketching may be done freehand, you may feel more comfortable using a parallel bar. Do not use a T-square; it is too difficult to use when rushed. Many of the Practicum exercises can be completed simply by marking the location of items on the plans provided and filling in informational boxes. Only the Space Planning, Egress, and Millwork exercises require standard drawings to be produced over a relatively large area of paper.

• architect's scale (imperial or metric depending on what scale is being used and where the exam is being given)

• 30°/60° and 45° triangles

• templates for shapes such as plumbing, furniture, and circles, including 1/8″ and 1/4″ ADA templates (only mass-produced templates may be used; homemade templates are not allowed)

- pencils and marking pens

- erasers (not electric)

- nonprogrammable, battery-operated calculator (make sure the batteries are fresh)

- pencil pointer and/or sharpener (manual)

- tracing paper (a 14 in (356 mm) wide roll is suitable; wider rolls are unnecessary and unwieldy)

- tape or drafting dots

- sticky notes and correction fluid (white-out)

Bring any other drawing tools that will make the work easier. For example, bring a variety of lead grades and types, as well as marking pens with different thicknesses, because the vellum supplied may be of varying quality that smears one type of marker but not another. In addition, consider taking "survival" items like the following.

- watch

- tissues

- snacks and bottled water (these are not allowed in the testing room, but can be consumed outside)

- aspirin

- eyedrops

- earplugs

WHAT TO DO AFTER THE EXAM

Score notifications for IDFX and IDPX will be sent within eight weeks after your test date. Score notifications for the Practicum will be sent within 14 weeks after your test date. If you pass the Practicum, you will receive a score report that indicates "Pass." If you fail the Practicum, you will receive a score report that indicates "Fail," along with a list of the exercises receiving failing scores. If you fail one or two of the three exam sections, you will only need to retake the failed section(s). Your state or province may impose restrictions on the number of years you can wait between taking different sections of the exam.

The council will issue you a certificate and a certificate number when you pass all three exam sections. The certificate number will be unique, and is used to distinguish designers within the interior design field. To identify yourself as an NCIDQ certificate holder on stationery, business cards, and so on, use the following format: "[First name] [Last name], NCIDQ® Certificate No. [######]." For example, "David Ballast, NCIDQ® Certificate No. 9425."

To maintain active status as an NCIDQ certificate holder, you must pay a yearly certificate renewal fee. You will receive your first renewal notice one year after your exam date.

PRACTICUM TIPS

Even if you are very familiar with the subject matter, taking the Practicum can be an arduous process simply because of its length and the concentration needed to get through it. As with any activity requiring endurance, it is important to be well rested for the exam. Stop studying a day or two before your exam day, relax as much as possible, and get plenty of sleep the night before.

Allow plenty of time to get to the exam site, in case of transportation problems such as getting lost or stuck in a traffic jam. Arrive at the exam room early to select a seat with good lighting, as far away from distractions as possible. Once you are in the room, arrange your working materials and other supplies and be prepared to begin as soon as you are allowed to. The proctor will review the exam instructions and general rules about breaks, smoking, permitted materials, and other housekeeping matters. Ask any questions about the rules at this time.

At the exam, seven 18″ × 24″ vellum drawing sheets will be provided to draw design solutions. The *NCIDQ Building Code Requirements*, which solutions must comply with, will also be given. Refer to the "What to Bring to the Exam" section in the Introduction for more information about what will be provided (and what to bring or leave at home) on exam day.

GENERAL GUIDELINES

Here are some guidelines for taking the Practicum. Guidelines for completing specific exercises are given in the following section, "Systematic Approaches to Solving the Exercises."

- Manage your time efficiently. The Practicum requires you to assimilate, analyze, and communicate a lot of information in a short amount of time.

- Remember that highly refined, drafted drawings are not required. Drawings may be freehand and may even be rather rough, as long as they show the graders that you have solved the exercise and your solution meets all of the project requirements.

- Read the instructions for each exercise quickly, complete the required drawing(s), and enter the required information into the tables provided on the drawing sheet. The code requirements will be given in each exercise's project requirements, but this information is also available ahead of time on the council's website, www.ncidq.org. You should also become thoroughly familiar with all the required code provisions, including accessibility requirements, before the exam.

- Keep in mind that each exercise is designed to test a specific area of knowledge and skill. Focus on that area and don't worry about other aspects of the design.

- Be careful not to read more into the exercise than is there. The examiners are very specific about what they want; there is no need to add to the exercise's requirements.

- Make liberal use of tracing paper to explore potential solutions. This is especially important for the Space Planning, Lighting Design, Egress, and Millwork exercises because there are many possible solutions for these. In other exercises, there may only be one or two correct solutions possible within the project requirements.

- Use only the code requirements given in the test booklets. These will most often follow the *International Building Code* (IBC) and be familiar, but may differ in a few instances. Read the *NCIDQ Building Code Requirements* before the exam and be very familiar with it.

- When you have a solution for an exercise, use the project statement as a checklist to check solutions to make sure every requirement has been satisfied.

- Relax as much as possible during study periods and during the exam itself. Worrying too much is counterproductive. If you have worked diligently in school, have obtained a wide range of work experience, and have started your exam review early, you will be in the best possible position to pass the exam.

SYSTEMATIC APPROACHES TO SOLVING THE EXERCISES

Use the following approaches for effective time management to complete the specific exercises in this practice exam, as well as on the actual Practicum.

Exercise 1: Space Planning

It can be difficult to manage your time during this exercise because there is much that has to be designed and shown on the drawing. At first glance, the number of spaces in the program requirements and the long list of furnishings and equipment required can seem daunting. But the exercise can be completed successfully by following a logical sequence of steps.

Step 1: Quickly add up the minimum areas for all the spaces given in the program. Compare this total with the area given on the base plan. The difference will show how much extra space is available for corridors and exceeding minimum areas.

Take the total program area and divide it by the area of the base plan. The resulting percentage will indicate how tightly the space must be planned. For example, if the total program area is 80% of the base plan area, you will know that you need to plan carefully; if it is only 65%, then there is more than enough space for circulation and for exceeding the programmed total for each space when necessary.

Step 2: The program will require a second means of egress. Determine an approximate location for the second means of egress so that there is a route from it to the primary entrance to the space. Depending on the base plan, this route may be a simple straight or

L-shaped corridor that serves all the spaces. Try not to create any dead-end corridors; however, if they are unavoidable, keep them as short as possible and in no case more than 20 ft (6.1 m) long.

Step 3: Make corridors 5 ft (1.5 m) wide. This will automatically create accessibility space for changes in direction, as well as maneuvering clearances on one side of every corridor door.

Step 4: Make sure the two exits are separated by at least the minimum required distance. For sprinklered buildings, this is one-third the maximum diagonal distance of the base plan. For non-sprinklered buildings, this is one-half the diagonal distance.

Step 5: On a piece of tracing paper, draw the boundaries within which plumbing may be placed to satisfy the program requirements. This may be a circle around an existing plumbing stack, or it may be two lines parallel to a line of plumbing shown on the base plan.

Step 6: Review the required adjacencies. Note any spaces that need to be close to plumbing. Also note any similar spaces that should be placed next to each other. With this information, block out a rough floor plan. The program requirements will say which spaces need to be near the entrance, which must have exterior windows, and which service spaces (closets, workrooms, storage rooms, and so on) do not require windows and can be located anywhere.

Do not attempt a plan that is complicated or that contains angled or curved partitions. Avoid shapes that take time to draw. The graders are not looking for innovative, award-winning solutions, just proof that you can respond to a program, work within the context of an existing building plan, and integrate health, safety, and welfare issues, as well as accessible design, into a two-dimensional solution.

Step 7: Look at your first rough plan and quickly check the areas of the spaces to make sure they meet the program requirements. If there is sufficient space in the base plan, make rooms a little larger than the required minimums. This will make it easier to fit the required furniture and equipment into the spaces and leave adequate accessibility maneuvering clearances. Make revisions as necessary to finalize the floor plan, being careful to locate doors so that there is at least 12 in (305 mm) of space on the push side and 18 in (457 mm) on the pull side. Be sure that all plumbing is within the distances prescribed by the program.

Step 8: Once the floor plan is finalized, begin placing furniture and equipment as required by the program. You must indicate the placement not only of furniture but of all small equipment, such as phones and computers. Draw the symbols for voice/data and power outlets in the spaces required by the program. Indicate the heights of any outlets drawn that deviate from the standard 18 in (457 mm) height. Note any receptacles near sinks and other plumbing that need to be ground fault interrupter outlets.

Step 9: Label each room with its name and area. Dimension the clearances of the egress paths and draw 5 ft (1.5 m) diameter dashed circles at changes in direction in the egress path. Draw accessible clearances at plumbing fixtures with dashed lines as well.

Exercise 2: Lighting Design

Like the Space Planning exercise, the Lighting Design exercise can be difficult because of the amount of information that must be analyzed in a short amount of time. The exercise gives 16 different luminaires that may be used and also specifies some general approach to the design, such as "dramatic" or "contrast of light and shadow." However, the design aspect is less important than meeting the watts per square foot (square meter) energy budget and switching the lights correctly.

Before the exam, review different lamp types and lamp wattages to understand how they compare with each other. LED lamps will be among the available luminaires, so be sure to understand their qualities, too. Table 1 lists the important characteristics of some common types of lamps. Figure 1 shows how these lamps compare in lumen output.

Table 1 Characteristics of Common Light Sources[a]

lamp description	initial luminous flux (lm)	efficacy (lm/W)	color temp. (K)	CRI	approx. lamp life (hr)
incandescent		5–20	2700–2800	100	750–4000
75W R-30	850	11	2500	100	2000
100W A-19	1750	17	2500	100	750
150W A-21	2810	19	2900	100	750
150W PAR 38	2200	12	2600	100	750
low voltage	560–850[b]	12–16	2800–3200	95–100	2000–10,000
50W MR-16	625	13	2800–3200	95	5000
75W MR-16	1200	16	3050	95	4000
tungsten-halogen		18–22	3000–3100	100	1000–4000
100W T-H PAR 38	2070	21	2900	100	2000
150W T-H PAR 38	2900	19	3000	100	3000
fluorescent		95–105	2700–7500	55–98	6000–24,000
F28T5 (4 ft)	2900	104	3000–6500	85	16,000
F32T8 (4 ft)	2950	92	3000–6500	85	20,000
old F40T12CW	3150	79	4300	62	20,000
F54T5HO (4 ft)	4400	71	2700–5000	82	20,000
compact fluorescent		25–85	2700–6500	82	8000–10,000
13W compact	900	70	2700–6500	82	12,000
24W GU-24	1600	60–70	2700–6500	80+	10,000–30,000
27W compact	1750	64	2700–6500	82	10,000
32W compact	2600	81	2700–6500	80+	10,000
TT-40W	3150	79	2700–6500	80+	12,000
mercury-vapor		20–60	5500–5900	15–52	14,000–25,000
100W DX A-23	4300	39	3700	45	24,000
metal-halide		35–100	3200–4300	65–85	5000–20,000
70W M-H	4900	70	3000	75	6000
70W ceramic metal-halide (CMH)	6000	80–100	3000–4100	80–90	15,000

(continued)

Table 1 Characteristics of Common Light Sources[a] (continued)

lamp description	initial luminous flux (lm)	efficacy (lm/W)	color temp. (K)	CRI	approx. lamp life (hr)
high-pressure sodium		80–140	1800–2800	22–70	10,000–24,000
35W T10	1250	36	2700	85	10,000
50W ED-17	2000	40	2700	85	10,000
LED			varies	varies	50,000–100,000
5W bi-pin	450	90	2700–6000	79	50,000
6W PAR 20	720	120	2700–6000	82	50,000
15W 4 ft tube	1500	100	2700–7500	80	50,000
64W 2 ft × 4 ft grid light	4800	75	2700–6000	80	50,000
72W wall wash unit	2040	28	2700–3200	82	50,000

(Multiply feet by 0.305 to obtain meters.)

[a]The values listed in the table are approximate and representative only. Individual manufacturers, ballasts, and lamps may provide different values.

[b]Because of their design, low-voltage MR lamps are rated on their center beam candlepower rather than lumens. This number is an approximation.

[c]Values for the efficacy of LEDs are difficult to compare with other sources because, as yet, there are no industry standard test procedures for rating the luminous flux of LED devices and arrays. Values are also expected to increase rapidly as improvements in LEDs take place.

Source: Compiled from various manufacturers' catalogs.

Figure 1 Lumen Output of Common Light Sources

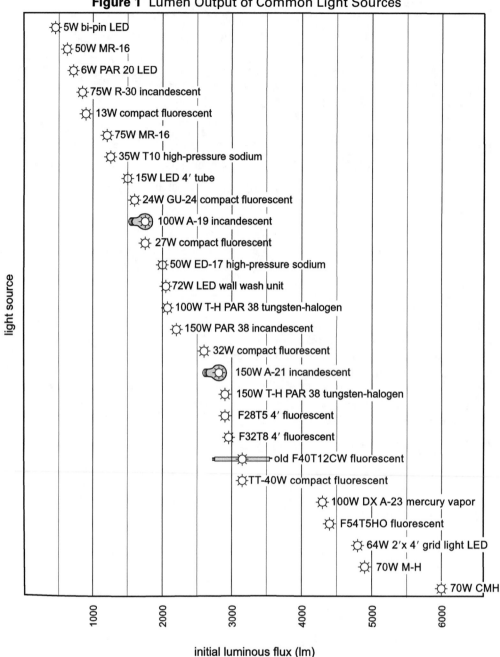

Source: Compiled from various manufacturers' catalogs.

During the exam, follow this suggested sequence of steps to complete the exercise in the time allotted.

Step 1: Go through the 16 luminaire cut sheets. Eliminate from consideration those that use standard incandescent lights with high wattages. One or two incandescent lamps in your solution may work, but if you use more than that, you are likely to exceed the energy budget or be limited to too few luminaires.

Also eliminate any wall sconces more than 4 in (100 mm) deep. ADA accessibility guidelines require that objects that extend from the wall more than 4 in (100 mm) be mounted at least

80 in (2030 mm) from the floor. Although you can indicate a mounting height greater than 80 in (2030 mm) on your drawing, placing wall sconces this high is rarely good lighting design unless the ceiling is high. Rather than spend time trying to make these fixtures work in your solution, it's easier to eliminate them from the start.

Step 2: Understand the general lighting requirements. The exercise will probably ask specifically for task lighting in one area. Use low-wattage downlights for this area and for other task lighting (such as undercounter lights) as appropriate. Other areas will require spot lighting for accents, wall washing, or display lighting. A few general ambient lights will also be necessary. Give your reason for selecting each type of luminaire in the notes area on the drawing sheet.

Select the appropriate low-wattage luminaire for each area and broad-spread luminaires for ambient lighting. Be careful not to overlight. The space in the problem will be fairly small and will not need to be heavily or elaborately lit.

Because lamps of different types must be switched separately, be careful to use similar lamps for similar functions, such as using compact fluorescents (for example) for all wall washing lights. To make this easier, use as few different types of luminaires as possible. If the space has a large daylighting component, consider using the daylight sensor switch symbol given. Also, be sure to use the correct switch symbol for each purpose—using a low-voltage dimmer, for example, for low-voltage luminaires. The program will require dimmer switches at certain areas.

Step 3: Dimension the lights where required. Note the mounting height of wall sconces, if you used them. Label one or two ambient lights for the night security light. Tag the lights with numbers, and fill in the lighting schedule. Calculate the wattage for each luminaire type, then add the wattages together and divide the total wattage by the given area. If you have used low-wattage lights throughout, the final value will probably be within the lighting budget. If it isn't, reduce the number of lights or take another look at the lamp wattages used and substitute another type of fixture.

Exercise 3: Egress

The Egress exercise is fairly straightforward. The most time-consuming aspect is simply putting all the required information on the answer sheet.

Step 1: Using tracing paper, measure and calculate the *actual* usable areas of the floor plan. You should make this calculation yourself because the area given for the entire building may be gross area and not useful for determining how much area will be needed for the suites given in the problem statement. Exclude from the calculation an allowance for a 5 ft (1.5 m) corridor around the core of the building leading to the exits. It will usually be easier to divide the floor plan into major sections and calculate them separately. The shape of the floor plan may suggest how to divide it; if not, the structural grid is a useful way to define these sections.

Step 2: Tentatively place the required suites on the base plan, using the required areas of the suites and the large chunks of area determined in the previous step. This should be done on tracing paper. Start with any space that is required by the program to be in a particular part of the plan; for example, one suite may require a northern exposure. Larger spaces are generally best placed in the corners of the building.

One space will require two exits; place this adjacent to a long enough stretch of public corridor so that the exits can be separated by at least the required distance. This is one-third or one-half the diagonal distance of the space, depending on whether the building is sprinklered or not.

Step 3: Adjust demising walls as needed to give each suite at least its minimum required area. Make sure demising walls intersect the exterior of the building at window mullions, columns, or solid walls.

Step 4: Place the doors that lead from the suites to the public corridor. Make sure that doors swing in the direction of travel and do not swing into the egress path. It is safe to make recessed entrances to the suites that are 3 ft (0.9 m) deep and 5 ft (1.5 m) wide. This gives room for the door swing and provides for accessible maneuvering clearance of 18 in (457 mm) on the pull side of the door. Use two exits for the suite that requires them. This is generally an assembly occupancy or an educational occupancy of some type of space with an occupant load greater than 49. Use the Occupancy Load Table given in the *NCIDQ Building Code Requirements* to determine when two exits are required.

Step 5: For the new space that requires two exits, draw the longest possible diagonal line across the space and dimension it. Then, draw a line joining the centers of the two exit doors and dimension it. The separation of the two doors must be at least the minimum required by the code requirements. If the building is sprinklered it must be one-third or more of the diagonal distance of the suite. If the building is non-sprinklered it must be one-half or more of the diagonal distance.

Step 6: Label each suite with its name, area, and occupant load. Calculate the occupant load for each suite by dividing its area by the occupant load factor taken from the Occupancy Load Table. For the area that will require two exits, be careful to use the smaller occupant load factor.

Step 7: Sum all the occupant loads, including that of the existing suite, and split this in two as evenly as possible to get the occupant loads for the two stairs. For example, if the total occupant load for the floor is 250, the occupant load for each stair will be 125; if the total is 251, the occupant loads for the stairs will be 125 and 126. Write the occupant loads for the stairs in the notes area as required.

Step 8: In the existing suite, determine the point that has the longest common path of egress travel. This will not necessarily be the point that is furthest from the exits; consider the path through the suite that connects the two exits, and look for the point that is furthest away from this path. Draw the common path of egress travel from this point and label the distance. The common path of egress travel is that portion of the exit access that the occupants are required to traverse before two separate and distinct paths of egress travel to two exits become available.

Step 9: Draw lines from the most remote point in the existing suite to each of the two exits. Measure these distances and label them. These are the maximum travel distances as required by the problem statement. Dimension the width of the public corridor and draw 5 ft (1.5 m) dashed circles at each change of egress direction to show accessibility.

Exercise 4: Life Safety

The Life Safety exercise can be difficult because there are so many different items that must be reviewed and placed on the drawing in a short time. The key to successfully completing this exercise is to focus on only one requirement at a time and work through them sequentially. Because the individual elements generally do not have a direct relationship with each other, the order is not critical; however, the following sequence of steps may be useful. Use the symbols given in the drawing legend on the floor plan sheet.

Step 1: Complete the partition schedule based on the requirements of the program. Generally, corridor walls, demising walls, and walls around any assembly area greater than 750 ft² (70 m²) must be fire rated. The program may suggest other partitions that have to be fire rated. Partitions around a secure area or an area requiring acoustic privacy must extend to the deck. If the program mentions acoustic privacy, make sure to mark the "yes" column for acoustical.

Step 2: Complete the door/frame/hardware schedule for doors tagged on the floor plan. Make all doors 7 ft (2134 mm) high. Use metal frames and solid-core doors when they occur in fire-rated partitions as determined in Step 1. Nonrated doors may have either aluminum frames or wood frames. However, most doors should be solid-core for durability and security in a commercial application. Using the requirements of the problem statement, select the appropriate hardware group. The requirements generally test on security, closer requirements (for exit doors), and appropriateness for double doors.

Step 3: Locate and draw exit signs, following the requirements in the problem statement. In most cases, wall-mounted exit signs should be located at all egress doors; if the way to an exit is not apparent, directional exit signs must point the way. For example, exit signs are generally not required from small spaces with only one door, but they are required in assembly areas and in larger areas. To locate them correctly, imagine standing in the space. Except in the case of a room with one door, you must be able to see an exit sign pointing toward the way out from anywhere within the space. Be sure to place at each stairway a directional sign pointing to the stairway door, so that someone could tell from a distance where the door is. Also, make sure the solid black portion of the symbol indicates where the illuminated portion should be.

Step 4: Locate and draw a smoke detector symbol in each room, corridor, and storage area. This includes the elevator lobby, public corridors, and public restrooms.

Step 5: Locate and draw audio/visual fire signal devices in all areas so that a device is visible from any location in the room or space. Normally, these devices should be mounted in corridors, the elevator lobby, restrooms, assembly rooms, and large spaces. They may be placed in private offices but are not required.

Step 6: Locate and draw the emergency lights in such a way that the path of egress travel receives light. This includes the egress path within the space as well as restrooms, the elevator lobby, and the public corridor. Individual rooms do not need emergency lighting.

Step 7: Determine how many fire extinguishers are required and place them so as to satisfy the code requirements. The program may give the minimum number required based on area and the maximum distance between the farthest occupant of the space and the fire extinguisher. Place one in the public corridor as well.

In all cases, make sure the requirements are met and all spaces are provided with the correct life safety equipment, but do not show excessive use of the equipment.

Exercise 5: Restroom (Washroom)

The Restroom (Washroom) exercise is one of the most straightforward of the exercises. In the amount of space given, only the required number of fixtures will fit. In the restroom, the accessible toilet stall should be located at the end of the space and the lavatories near the entrance. All the plumbing fixtures must be along the plumbing chase. These requirements leave very little flexibility in the layout, and the exercise is one of making sure the correct space is provided for each fixture and all necessary dimensions are included. Be sure to dimension to the centerlines of fixtures as well as any partitions used. The accessories must be shown and the grab bars must be drawn to scale.

Step 1: Show accessible spaces with dashed lines, using the dimensions given in the project building code requirements. This should include 5 ft (1.5 m) turning circles and accessible space at lavatories, urinals, tubs, or other fixtures where they are required.

Step 2: Complete the fixture and accessory schedule, and note the mounting heights of the fixtures as given in the program or as required for accessibility. There must be exactly as many tags on the fixture schedule as there are on the list of fixtures in the program.

Step 3: Complete the notes section. Keep things simple and indicate cementitious backer board with ceramic tile finish.

Exercise 6: Systems Integration

The most difficult part of this exercise is locating the conflicts and proposing the best way to resolve them. To view the construction, place one sheet of vellum over the other to line up the floor plans. Place the reflected ceiling plan over the mechanical plan because this makes the grayed-out furniture easier to see. After doing this, use these steps to help you complete the exercise efficiently.

Step 1: Sketch all the elements to scale in section view in order to see the vertical relationships among them. A standard, single-view section is not necessary; a composite view is needed that shows all the elements to scale at their given heights above the floor. On this sketch, the individual elements may overlap one another.

Step 2: Lay a piece of tracing paper over the wall section and trace the floors and structural elements first. Then draw the two ceiling heights, one on each half of the sketch.

Step 3: Draw a rectangle representing the main HVAC trunk duct, and assume that it is placed as high as possible, almost touching the lowest structural element it passes under. Then draw lines representing the height of the branch duct or ducts. When ductwork is shown on the plans, the dimensions for the duct represent the width of the duct first and then the height. For example, an indication of 16″ × 12″ (400 mm × 300 mm) on the mechanical plan is a duct 16 in (400 mm) wide and 12 in (300 mm) high.

Step 4: For sprinkler pipes, both the trunk line and branch lines, draw circles about 3 in (75 mm) in diameter using the heights given on the mechanical and sprinkler plan. Assume the heights given are to the bottoms of the pipes. At this point, it should become clear where sprinkler lines and ductwork will be in conflict when they cross on the mechanical plan.

Step 5: Draw rectangles representing the luminaires, using the heights given on the lighting schedule. This will make it clear where lights will be in conflict with ducts and pipes when they are in the same location on the plan. Draw any pendent or suspended lights and note their lengths and heights above the floor.

Step 6: With the floor plans superimposed and the study sketch at hand, look at each clouded area to find the conflict. It should be fairly obvious where ducts and sprinkler pipes conflict and where ducts and light fixtures conflict. Recessed lights may also conflict with air handling units. Notice all cases of two items in the same place, such as a sprinkler head and light fixture in the same ceiling grid or a track light overlapping an air diffuser or return air grille. Thermostats may be placed incorrectly behind furniture or equipment; relocate these as necessary.

As you discover each conflict, write it on the notes schedule along with the proposed solution. If appropriate, draw the suggested solution on the reflected ceiling plan. Be sure not to modify anything that is specifically prohibited by the problem statement, such as trunk lines or furniture. Do not add or delete light fixtures or HVAC equipment.

Step 7: Draw an access door, if required, near the main mechanical unit, and indicate the depth and mounting height of wall sconces on the lighting schedule. Give a depth of 4 in (100 mm) to meet accessibility requirements; a mounting height from 60 in to 66 in (1520 mm to 1680 mm) is adequate.

Exercise 7: Millwork

The Millwork exercise tests your knowledge not only of millwork construction but also of coordination with plumbing and electrical services and accessibility. The exercise requires drawing a plan, elevation, and section of a relatively small portion of millwork that must include provisions for accessibility. The exercise can be completed using the following steps.

Step 1: Draw the plan view first, being careful to satisfy the program requirements for size, location relative to plumbing and electrical services, and clearances for accessibility adjacent to existing construction. The program requirements are fairly specific and, given the existing space within which the millwork must be placed, there will be only one or two ways to lay the plan out correctly. The plan must show dimensions, clearances for accessibility, and any accessible electrical receptacles or other accessible items. An elevation and section cut symbol must also be drawn to refer to the respective elevation and section.

Step 2: Draw the elevation. (You could draw either the section or elevation, but you will probably see things better by starting with the elevation.) Use the elevation to work out the height of the countertops and the locations of any shelving or other required millwork items, electrical receptacles, and plumbing. Your elevation must include dimensions for constructability, notes on at least two appropriate finish materials (including the countertops), and dimensions for the accessible sink or other accessible feature given in the program.

Step 3: Show a portion of construction through the sink or other accessible feature. You must indicate that the element is accessible, and you must also indicate other millwork construction, including substrates and how the millwork item is constructed.

HOW SI UNITS ARE USED IN THIS BOOK

This book uses customary U.S. units (also called English or inch-pound units) as the primary measuring system and includes equivalent measurements in the text and illustrations, using the Système International d'Unités (SI), commonly called the metric system. The use of SI units for construction and publishing in the United States is problematic because the building construction industry (with the exception of federal construction) has generally not adopted metric units. Equivalent measurements of customary U.S. units are usually given as *soft* conversions, whereas customary U.S. measurements are simply converted into SI units using standard conversion factors. This results in a number with excessive significant digits. When construction is done using SI units, the building is designed and drawn according to *hard* conversions, where planning dimensions and building products are based on a metric module from the beginning. For example, studs are spaced 400 mm on center to accommodate panel products that are manufactured in standard 1200 mm widths.

As the United States transitions to using SI units, code-writing bodies, federal laws (such as the Americans with Disabilities Act, or ADA), product manufacturers, trade associations, and other construction-related industries typically still use the customary U.S. system and make soft conversions to develop SI equivalents. Some manufacturers produce the same product using both measuring systems. Although there are industry standards for developing SI equivalents, there is no consistent method in use for rounding off conversions. For example, the *International Building Code* (IBC) shows a 152 mm equivalent when a 6 in dimension is required. The *Americans with Disabilities Act and Architectural Barriers Act Accessibility Guidelines* (*ADA/ABA Guidelines*) gives a 150 mm equivalent for the same customary U.S. dimension.

To further complicate matters, each publisher may employ a slightly different house style in handling SI equivalents when customary U.S. units are used as the primary measuring system. The confusion is likely to continue until the U.S. construction industry adopts the SI system completely, precluding the need for dual dimensioning in publishing.

For the purposes of this book, the following conventions have been adopted.

• When dimensions are for informational use, the SI equivalent rounded to the nearest millimeter is used.

• When dimensions relate to planning or design guidelines, the SI equivalent is rounded to the nearest 5 mm for numbers over a few inches and to the nearest 10 mm for numbers over a few feet. When the dimension exceeds several feet, the number is rounded to the nearest 100 mm. For example, if a given activity requires a space about 10 ft wide, the modular, rounded SI equivalent will be given as 3000 mm. More exact conversions are not required.

• When an item is manufactured only to a customary U.S. measurement, the nearest SI equivalent rounded to the nearest millimeter is given, unless the dimension is very small (as for metal gages), in which case a more precise decimal equivalent will be given. Some materials, such as glass, are often manufactured to SI sizes. For example, a nominal $^1/_2$ in thick piece of glass will have an SI equivalent of 13 mm but can be ordered as 12 mm.

• When there is a hard conversion in the industry and an SI equivalent item is manufactured, the hard conversion is given. For example, a 24 in × 24 in ceiling tile would have the hard conversion of 600 mm × 600 mm (instead of 610 mm) because this size is manufactured and available in the United States.

• When an SI conversion is given in reference to a code, such as the IBC, or a regulation, such as the *ADA/ABA Guidelines*, the SI equivalent used in that code or regulation is also given in this book. For example, the same 10 ft dimension given previously as 3000 mm for a planning guideline would have a building code SI equivalent of 3048 mm because this is what the IBC requires. The *ADA/ABA Guidelines* generally follow the rounding rule of taking SI dimensions to the nearest 10 mm. For example, a 10 ft requirement for accessibility will be shown as 3050 mm. The code requirements for readers outside the United States may be slightly different.

• Throughout this book, the customary U.S. measurements are given first and the SI equivalents follow in parentheses. In text, SI units are always given. For example, a dimension might be indicated as 4 ft 8 in (1420 mm). In illustrations, however, standard convention is followed; the SI equivalent is usually without units and is assumed to be in millimeters unless other units are given. The same measurement in an illustration would appear as 4′ 8″ (1420).

CODES, STANDARDS, AND REFERENCES FOR THE EXAM

CODES AND STANDARDS
The Practicum covers information related to the following codes and standards.

IBC: *International Building Code, 2012*. International Code Council. Washington, DC.

ADA/ABA Guidelines: Americans with Disabilities Act and Architectural Barriers Act Accessibility Guidelines. U.S. Access Board, Washington, DC. www.access-board.gov/ada-aba/final.cfm.

REFERENCES
The following references contain information about the interior design field, including information specific to Practicum content areas. These references may be useful to review as you prepare for the exam.

Ballast, David Kent. *Interior Construction and Detailing for Designers and Architects*. Belmont, CA: PPI.

————. *Interior Design Reference Manual: Everything You Need to Know to Pass the NCIDQ Exam*. Belmont, CA: PPI.

Binggeli, Corky. *Building Systems for Interior Designers*. Hoboken, NJ: John Wiley and Sons.

Ching, Francis D. K., and Corky Binggeli. *Interior Design Illustrated*. Hoboken, NJ: John Wiley and Sons.

Ching, Francis D. K., and Steven R. Winkel. *Building Codes Illustrated: A Guide to Understanding the 2012 International Building Code*. Hoboken, NJ: John Wiley and Sons.

Coleman, Cindy, ed. *Interior Design Handbook of Professional Practice*. New York, NY: McGraw-Hill Professional Publishing.

Gordon, Gary. *Interior Lighting for Designers*. Hoboken, NJ: John Wiley and Sons.

Grondzik, Walter T., Benjamin Stein, Alison G. Kwok, and John S. Reynolds. *Mechanical and Electrical Equipment for Buildings*. Hoboken, NJ: John Wiley and Sons.

Harmon, Sharon Koomen, and Katherine E. Kennon. *The Codes Guidebook for Interiors.* Hoboken, NJ: John Wiley and Sons.

Karlen, Mark. *Space Planning Basics.* Hoboken, NJ: John Wiley and Sons.

Kilmer, W. Otie and Rosemary Kilmer. *Construction Drawings and Details for Interiors: Basic Skills.* Hoboken, NJ: John Wiley and Sons.

McGowan, Maryrose, and Kelsey Kruse, eds. *Interior Graphic Standards.* Hoboken, NJ: John Wiley and Sons.

Piotrowski, Christine M. *Professional Practice for Interior Designers.* Hoboken, NJ: John Wiley and Sons.

Reznikoff, S. C. *Interior Graphic and Design Standards.* New York, NY: Whitney Library of Design.

————. *Specifications for Commercial Interiors: Professional Liabilities, Regulations, and Performance Criteria.* New York, NY: Whitney Library of Design.

Riggs, J. Rosemary. *Materials and Components of Interior Architecture.* Upper Saddle River, NJ: Prentice Hall.

U.S. Green Building Council. *LEED Reference Guide for Green Interior Design and Construction.* Washington, DC: U.S. Green Building Council.

EXERCISE BUILDING CODE REQUIREMENTS

Your exercise solutions must comply with the requirements listed in this section. While the code requirements listed here are similar to the *NCIDQ Building Code Requirements*, the following code requirements are for the purposes of this practice examination only and may be different from what is presented in the NCIDQ document.[1]

DEFINITIONS

1. *Common path of egress travel:* That portion of the exit access that must be traversed before two separate and distinct paths of travel to two exits are available. The common path of egress travel shall be included within the permitted travel distance.

2. *Travel distance:* The distance measured from the most remote point within a story to the entrance to an exit along the natural and unobstructed path of egress travel.

FIRE-RESISTANT RATED CONSTRUCTION

1. Partitions along a public corridor must be 1-hour fire rated.

2. Demising partitions between tenant spaces must be 1-hour fire rated.

3. Partitions that demise an assembly occupancy of 750 ft^2 (70 m^2) or greater must be 1-hour fire rated.

4. Door assemblies in a 1-hour fire rated partition must have a minimum fire protection rating of 20 minutes and be self-closing.

---

[1]Prior to taking the actual exam, review the *NCIDQ Building Code Requirements* at www.ncidq.org. At the Practicum, a copy of the requirements will be provided in the exam booklet. Scores are based on how well solutions comply with the *NCIDQ Building Code Requirements* in order to protect the health, safety, and welfare of the public.

FIRE PROTECTION SYSTEMS

1. There must be an audio/visual fire signal device located in each restroom, hallway, lobby, and general assembly area.

2. An audio/visual fire signal device must be visible from any location in the room or space and must be mounted between 6 ft 8 in and 7 ft 6 in (2 m and 2.3 m) above finish floor (AFF).

3. The minimum number of fire extinguishers must be calculated based on one (1) fire extinguisher per 3000 ft^2 (280 m^2).

4. Fire extinguishers must be located no more than 75 ft (23 m) from the furthest occupant.

5. Smoke and heat detector coverage must include all rooms, corridors, storage areas, and spaces above suspended ceilings.

MEANS OF EGRESS

General Means of Egress

1. The means of egress must have a ceiling height of not less than 7 ft 6 in (2.3 m).

2. Protruding objects must not reduce the minimum clear width of accessible routes.

3. All objects located on a wall between 27 in (685 mm) and 80 in (2115 mm) AFF must not protrude more than 4 in (100 mm) into an egress path of travel.

Exit Signs

1. Exit signs with a directional indicator (illuminated) showing the direction of travel shall be placed in every location where the direction of travel to reach the nearest exit is not apparent.

Illumination

1. Emergency illumination shall be provided for a minimum of 1 $^1/_2$ hours in the event of failure of normal lighting. Emergency lighting facilities shall be arranged to provide initial illumination along the path of egress at floor level.

Travel Distance

1. All paths of travel must be accessible (barrier-free) and provide at minimum a 60 in (1500 mm) turning radius at changes of travel direction.

2. The path of egress travel must not pass through a secondary space that is subject to closure by doors or that contains storage materials or has items that project into the path of travel.

3. The common path of travel distance must not exceed 75 ft (23 m).

4. The travel distance to an exit must be measured on the floor along the centerline of the natural path of travel, starting from the most remote point to the centerline of the exit.

5. The travel distance must not exceed 250 ft (76.2 m) measured along the path of travel.

Exit Access Doors, Doorways, Door Hardware, and Windows

1. The height of doors must not be less than 7 ft (2.1 m).

2. All door openings shall be a minimum of 36 in (900 mm) wide with an 18 in (450 mm) clear space on the pull side of the door and a 12 in (300 mm) clear space on the push side of the door.

3. Where a pair of doors is provided, one of the doors must be not less than 36 in (900 mm) wide.

4. Locks, if provided, must not require the use of a key, special knowledge, or effort for operation from the egress side.

5. Doors opening from occupied spaces into the path of egress travel shall not project more than 7 in (180 mm) into the required width.

6. Exit access doorways must open in the direction of exit travel.

7. Exit access doorways must be placed at a distance that is equal to or greater than

   (a) when the building is not sprinklered, one-half the length of the maximum overall diagonal dimension of the area being served, measured in a straight line between exit doors or exit access doorways;

   (b) when the building is sprinklered, one-third the length of the maximum overall diagonal dimension of the area being served, measured in a straight line between exit doors or exit access doorways.

8. Two (2) exit access doorways must be provided from any space where the occupancy load exceeds 49 in occupancy groups A (assembly), B (business), and M (mercantile) or exceeds 29 in occupancy group S (storage).

Corridors

1. The minimum interior corridor width must be 44 in (1100 mm).

2. Dead-end corridors must not exceed 20 ft (6 m) in length.

ACCESSIBILITY

1. Service counters (reception/transaction) over 8 ft (2.4 m) in length must have an accessible height service counter, a minimum of 26 in (900 mm) in length.

2. All accessible (barrier-free) countertops, sinks, reception/transaction surfaces, and other horizontal work surfaces must not exceed 34 in (865 mm) AFF with a 27 in high (685 mm) clear knee space below.

3. All accessible (barrier-free) counters must have clear knee space of at least 30 in wide × 17 in deep (760 mm wide × 430 mm deep).

4. All exposed hot water pipes and drains must be insulated or otherwise protect wheelchair users from burns on the legs.

5. All accessible (barrier-free) wall-mounted controls must be located between 15 in (380 mm) and 48 in (1200 mm) AFF for a forward reach and between 9 in (230 mm) and 54 in (1370 mm) AFF for a side reach.

6. All accessible (barrier-free) lower cabinets must have a 3 in deep × 8 in high (75 mm deep × 200 mm high) toe-kick.

7. All accessible (barrier-free) upper cabinets or shelves located above a work surface must not exceed 48 in (1200 mm) AFF.

8. Restrooms

   • All accessible toilets must have an unobstructed 60 in (1500 mm) turning circle.

   • Accessible toilets must be mounted at 18 in (450 mm) AFF to the top of the toilet seat.

   • All grab bars at toilets must be 36 in (900 mm) long at the rear and 42 in (1060 mm) long at the side, mounted between 33 in (840 mm) and 36 in (900 mm) AFF.

   • Accessible urinals must have an elongated rim at a maximum height of 17 in (430 mm) AFF.

   • A clear floor space of 30 in × 48 in (760 mm × 1200 mm) must be provided in front of accessible lavatories and urinals.

   • Accessible mirrors must be mounted with the bottom edge of the reflective surface no higher than 40 in (1000 mm) AFF.

STRUCTURAL

1. Core drills must not be within 18 in (450 mm) of any structural element.

ELECTRICAL

1. All electrical receptacles must be 18 in (450 mm) AFF unless otherwise noted in program requirements.

2. All electrical receptacles located within 36 in (900 mm) of a water source must be ground fault interrupters (GFI).

3. Clearance of 36 in (900 mm) deep must be provided in front of power panels.

Table 1 Occupancy Load Table

function of space	floor area in ft^2 (m^2) per occupant
accessory storage areas and mechanical equipment rooms	300 (28) gross
assembly without fixed seats	
concentrated (chairs only—not fixed)	7 (0.7) net
standing space	5 (0.5) net
unconcentrated (tables and chairs)	15 (1.4) net
business areas	100 (9.3) gross
education	
classroom area	20 (1.9) net
shops and other vocational room areas	50 (4.6) net
exercise rooms	50 (4.6) gross
kitchens, commercial	200 (18.6) gross
mercantile	
basement and grade floor areas	30 (2.8) gross
areas on other floors	60 (5.6) gross
storage, stock, shipping areas	300 (28) gross
residential	200 (18.6) gross (two (2) persons per sleeping room)

PART A

INSTRUCTIONS

You will have four (4) hours in which to work the following two exercises.

- Exercise 1: Space Planning
- Exercise 2: Lighting Design

To complete these exercises, you will need

- Exercise Building Code Requirements
- Worksheet ID-1 (floor plan)
- Worksheet ID-2a (floor plan)
- Worksheet ID-2b (reflected ceiling plan)

For each exercise, you will be given a project description, project requirements, and required design instructions. Complete each solution on the appropriate worksheet. Thumbnails of the worksheet or worksheets you will need are shown at the beginning of each exercise. As with the actual exam, reference materials are not permitted. Only this book's Exercise Building Code Requirements may be used.

If you finish Part A before the allotted time is up, check your solutions to make sure you've met all the project and building code requirements. On the actual exam, your solutions will be graded based on your ability to meet the required project and building code requirements, as well as your ability to demonstrate the level of knowledge and skill required to protect public health, safety, and welfare.

EXERCISE 1: SPACE PLANNING
PROJECT DESCRIPTION AND REQUIREMENTS

Project Description

The administration offices of a small urban college are being moved into a new space as shown on worksheet ID-1. The college intends to expand the office space in the future and has taken an option on the current tenant space to the north between grid lines 1 and 2. Planning for the new space should account for this option to allow for ease of expansion.

The area of work is a tenant space in the southwest corner of a mid-rise building. The building is fully sprinklered. The space is approximately 2660 ft² (247 m²). All windowsill heights are 30 in (760 mm) AFF. Available plumbing is located along column B2.

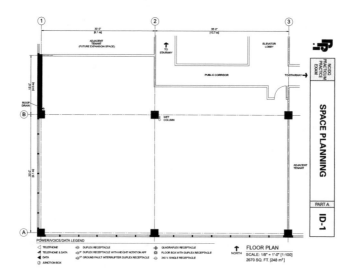

Project Requirements

1. Primary adjacencies

    • Advising and Reception

    • Secretary and Dean and Assistant dean

    • Secretary and Clerk

2. Secondary adjacencies

    • Conference and Reception

    • Work/copy room and File room

3. Plumbing and partition requirements

    • All plumbing must be located within 10 ft (3.1 m) of the wet column.

    • All new partitions intersecting the exterior wall must fall on window mullions or along a column.

Program Requirements

space name	qty.	minimum area ft² (m²)	function	minimum equipment
Reception	1	350 (32.5)	reception station for one (1) staff member, with 36 in (900 mm) high transaction counter; area planned so as to divert people entering to either the advising area or to the offices	one (1) PC one (1) phone one (1) four-drawer lateral file or two (2) two-drawer files, 42 in (1067 mm) wide one (1) printer/fax 6 linear ft (1.82 m) of counter top seating for three (3) people and one (1) wheelchair with side table wall-hung literature rack, 36 in wide × 48 in high × 4 in deep (900 mm wide × 1200 mm high × 100 mm deep)
Coat closet	1	10 (0.9)	coat closet for staff and visitors	one rod and shelf
Advising	2	150 (13.9)	private office	one (1) PC one (1) telephone two (2) visitor's chairs two (2) two-drawer lateral files, 36 in (915 mm) wide
Conference	1	300 (27.9)	seating for eight (8) people	one (1) conference table minimum of 42 in (1067 mm) wide one (1) credenza, 18 in × 72 in (457 mm × 1830 mm)
Dean	1	225 (20.9)	dean's private office	one (1) PC one (1) phone
Assistant dean	1	150 (13.9)	assistant dean's private office	one (1) PC one (1) phone
Secretary	1	150 (13.9)	open to corridor	one (1) PC one (1) phone one (1) four-drawer lateral file, 42 in (1067 mm) wide
Clerk	1	100 (9.3)	open to corridor with desk or workstation	one (1) PC one (1) phone one (1) four-drawer lateral file, 42 in (1067 mm) wide
File room	1	125 (11.6)	lockable room	six (6) four-drawer lateral files, 42 in (1067 mm) wide

(continued)

(continued)

space name	qty.	minimum area ft² (m²)	function	minimum equipment
Work/copy room	1	150 (13.9)	copy machine and space for collating and binding reports and other documents; general work area	one copy machine requiring an area 72 in wide and 42 in deep (1830 mm wide × 1067 mm deep); copy machine requires 240 V electrical service
				8 linear ft (2.4 m) of countertop
				minimum of 8 linear ft (2.4 m) of upper and base cabinets
				one (1) tabletop electric binding machine, 10 in wide × 6 in high × 14 in deep (255 mm wide × 150 mm high × 355 mm deep)
Coffee/lounge	1	150 (13.9)	staff lunchroom and break room	seating for four (4)
				8 linear ft (2.4 m) of countertop with sink
				minimum of 8 linear ft (2.4 m) of upper and base cabinets
				one (1) undercounter refrigerator
				one (1) coffee maker
				one (1) microwave
Men's room	1	64 (6)	single user, accessible	one (1) toilet
				one (1) lavatory
				grab bars as required by code
				one (1) mirror
				one (1) soap dispenser, 4 in wide × 12 in high × 4 in deep (100 mm wide × 300 mm high × 100 mm deep)
				one (1) hand dryer, 12 in wide × 12 in high × 8 in deep (300 mm wide × 300 mm high × 200 mm deep)
				one (1) trash receptacle

(continued)

(continued)

space name	qty.	minimum area ft² (m²)	function	minimum equipment
Women's room	1	64 (6)	single user, accessible	one (1) toilet
				one (1) lavatory
				grab bars as required by code
				one (1) mirror
				one (1) soap dispenser, 4 in wide × 12 in high × 4 in deep (100 mm wide × 300 mm high × 100 mm deep)
				one (1) hand dryer, 12 in wide × 12 in high × 8 in deep (300 mm wide × 300 mm high × 200 mm deep)
				one (1) trash receptacle
Telephone/ server	1	15 (1.4)	lockable area for telephone board and computer server	one (1) telephone panel, 36 in (900 mm) wide
				one (1) server rack, 24 in (600 mm) wide

Required Design Solution

For this exercise, use the information given on worksheet ID-1. Be familiar with the floor plan and project description and aware of any physical constraints of the building shell.

Instructions to Candidate

1. Design a solution for the space on the floor plan meeting all requirements. All elements must be shown at the appropriate scale.

2. Limit solution to the area of the work on the floor plan.

3. Comply with all applicable codes as given in the Exercise Building Code Requirements.

4. Comply with the following drawing requirements.

    - Label each room with room name and area in square feet (square meters).

    - Provide one additional means of egress from the demised area. Do not go through adjacent tenant spaces. Add the additional egress door anywhere along the public corridor.

    - Draw all casework, equipment, and plumbing fixtures, including the minimum requirements listed in the program requirements.

    - Fully furnish the space, using the minimum requirements listed in the program requirements and general knowledge for what would be necessary for this tenant's business. It is not mandatory to label or tag furniture. If not tagged, the furniture should be appropriately scaled and recognizable as what it is (seating, desk, and so on).

    - Dimension circulation clearances. Draw barrier-free clearances at critical changes in direction. Draw barrier-free clearances at accessible plumbing fixtures as indicated in the program requirements. Dimension egress corridor widths.

5. Comply with the following power/voice/data requirements.

    - Using the symbols from the power/voice/data legend, indicate power, voice, and data required for the

        –Dean's office

        –Coffee/lounge

        –Work/copy room

    - Assume a receptacle mounting height of 18 in (457 mm) AFF. On the drawing, note any mounting height on any outlets that vary from this standard. Also note GFI on receptacles as required in the building code requirements.

EXERCISE 2: LIGHTING DESIGN
PROJECT DESCRIPTION AND REQUIREMENTS

Project Description

The area of work is a small visitor's center located on the ground level of a historic building at the edge of a state park. The center contains displays that show the history and ecology of the park. The center also sells books and other items related to the area.

The visitor's center has been designed as shown on worksheet ID-2a. The ceiling is suspended gypsum wallboard as shown on worksheet ID-2b, with the ceiling heights as indicated on the drawing.

Recognizing that electrical engineers are often required for lighting design, this exercise is designed to demonstrate the ability to develop a preliminary design and to effectively communicate design intent with respect to lighting design and controls within the boundaries of code compliance.

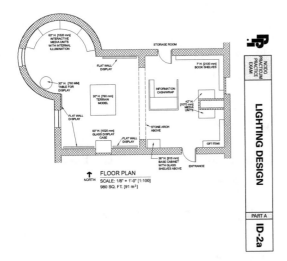

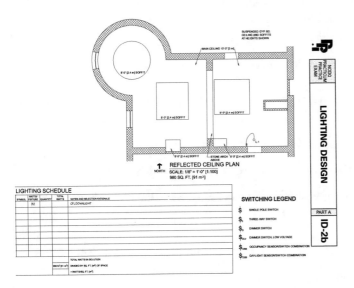

Project Requirements

Accommodate the following lighting criteria.

- general ambient lighting for the visitor's center

- appropriate high-end lighting solution that uses drama and contrast of light and shadow, while still providing the appropriate levels and types of illumination for displays

- task lighting for the cash/wrap area

- accent lighting for the terrain model and flat wall displays

- adjustable levels of illumination at displays

- energy allowance of 1.5 W/ft^2 (15 W/m^2)

Required Design Solution

For this exercise, use the plans and information given on worksheets ID-2a and ID-2b and only the fixtures given on the cut sheets provided in Fig. 2.1.

Instructions to Candidate

1. Design lighting and switching solutions for the area of work shown in the plans, using fixtures from the cut sheets provided in Fig. 2.1.

2. Use energy-efficient design principles and switching, considering energy trade-offs as adjusted to this occupancy type and use.

3. Comply with all applicable codes as indicated in the Exercise Building Code Requirements.

4. Using the lighting symbols on the cut sheets, draw the lighting plan on the reflected ceiling plan (worksheet ID-2b).

    - Label lighting fixtures with tag numbers as indicated on the cut sheets in Fig. 2.1.

    - Designate an appropriate fixture as a nighttime security light, and indicate with the letters NL adjacent to the fixture symbol on the plan.

    - Dimension fixture locations in the soffit over the cash/wrap.

    - Note mounting height for wall sconces.

5. Using the switching legend shown on the plan, draw the switching plan on the reflected ceiling plan (worksheet ID-2b).

    - Switch general ambient, task, and accent lighting separately.

    - Switch light sources (incandescent, fluorescent, halogen, LED, etc.) separately.

    - Connect all lighting fixtures that are to be operated by a single switch with a curved line.

6. Complete the lighting schedule on the reflected ceiling plan (worksheet ID-2b).

    - Note the selection rationale.

    - Summarize wattage.

Figure 2.1 Lighting Specifications

L-1

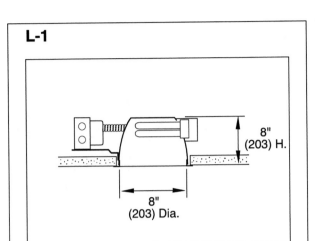

Symbol: ◯
L-1

Description: Compact fluorescent downlight
Total wattage: 32 W
Lamp: Triple-tube CFL
Dimensions: 8" Dia. × 8" H.

L-2

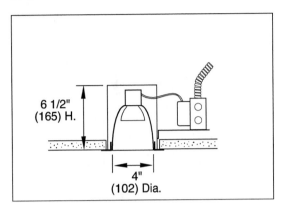

Symbol: ◯
L-2

Description: Low-voltage downlight
Total wattage: 75 W
Lamp: MR-16
Dimensions: 4" Dia. × 6 1/2" H.

L-3

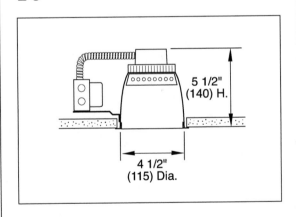

Symbol: ◯
L-3

Description: LED downlight
Total wattage: 24 W
Lamp: High-output LED
Dimensions: 4 1/2" Dia. × 5 1/2" H.

L-4

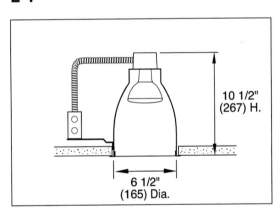

Symbol: ◯
L-4

Description: Incandescent downlight
Total wattage: 150 W
Lamp: (1) PAR 38
Dimensions: 6 1/2" Dia. × 10 1/2" H.

(continued)

Figure 2.1 Lighting Specifications (continued)

L-5

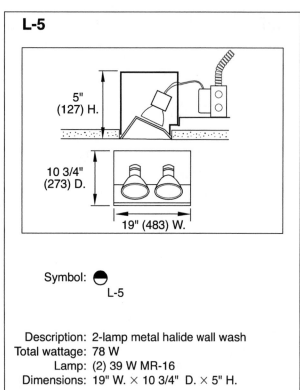

Symbol: L-5

Description: 2-lamp metal halide wall wash
Total wattage: 78 W
Lamp: (2) 39 W MR-16
Dimensions: 19" W. × 10 3/4" D. × 5" H.

L-6

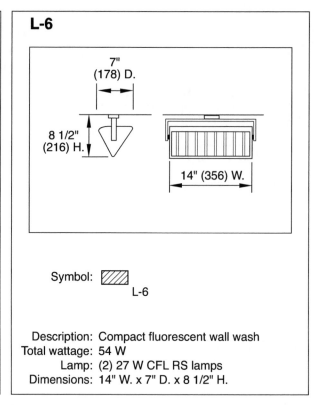

Symbol: L-6

Description: Compact fluorescent wall wash
Total wattage: 54 W
Lamp: (2) 27 W CFL RS lamps
Dimensions: 14" W. x 7" D. x 8 1/2" H.

L-7

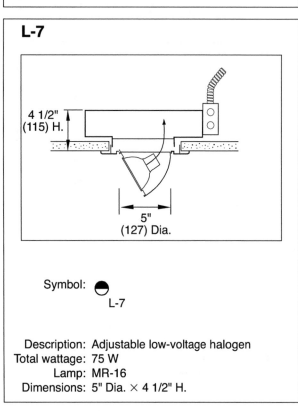

Symbol: L-7

Description: Adjustable low-voltage halogen
Total wattage: 75 W
Lamp: MR-16
Dimensions: 5" Dia. × 4 1/2" H.

L-8

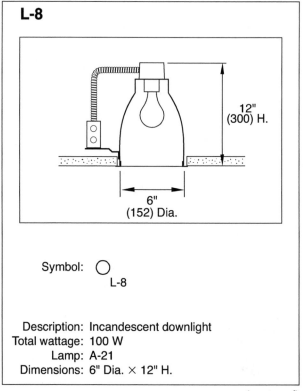

Symbol: L-8

Description: Incandescent downlight
Total wattage: 100 W
Lamp: A-21
Dimensions: 6" Dia. × 12" H.

(continued)

Figure 2.1 Lighting Specifications (continued)

L-9

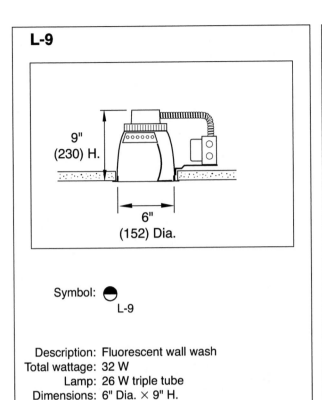

Symbol: L-9

Description: Fluorescent wall wash
Total wattage: 32 W
Lamp: 26 W triple tube
Dimensions: 6" Dia. × 9" H.

L-10

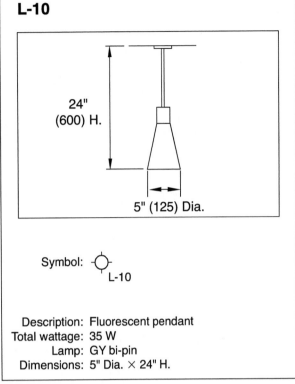

Symbol: L-10

Description: Fluorescent pendant
Total wattage: 35 W
Lamp: GY bi-pin
Dimensions: 5" Dia. × 24" H.

L-11

Symbol: L-11

Description: Fluorescent wall sconce
Total wattage: 26 W
Lamp: Quad. CFL
Dimensions: 14" W. × 4" D. × 16" H.

L-12

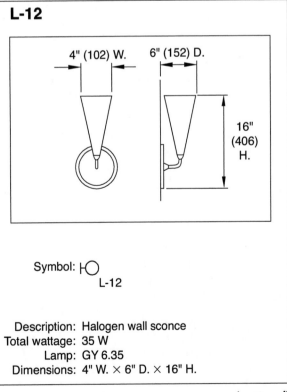

Symbol: L-12

Description: Halogen wall sconce
Total wattage: 35 W
Lamp: GY 6.35
Dimensions: 4" W. × 6" D. × 16" H.

(continued)

Figure 2.1 Lighting Specifications (continued)

L-13

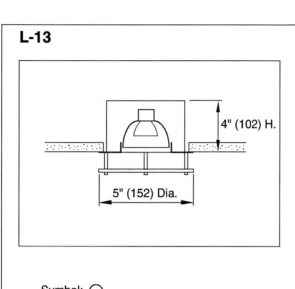

Symbol: ◯
L-13

Description: Low voltage
Total wattage: 75 W
Lamp: MR-16
Dimensions: 5" Dia. × 4" H.

L-14

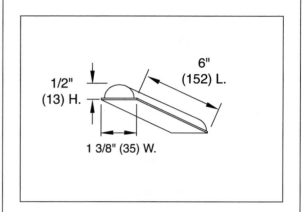

Symbol: ▬ ▬ ▬ ▬ ▬
L-14

Description: Linear LED display case light
Total wattage: 5 W per foot
Lamp: LED
Dimensions: 1 3/8" W. × 1/2" H. × 6" L. each segment

L-15

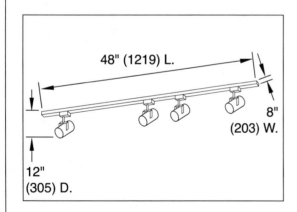

Symbol:
L-15

Description: Incandescent track light
Total wattage: 240 W
Lamp: (4) 60 W halogen
Dimensions: 8" W. × 12" D. × 48" L.

L-16

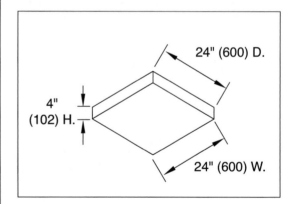

Symbol:
L-16

Description: Surface-mounted fluorescent
Total wattage: 64 W
Lamp: (2) T8 U6
Dimensions: 24" W. × 24" D. × 4" H.

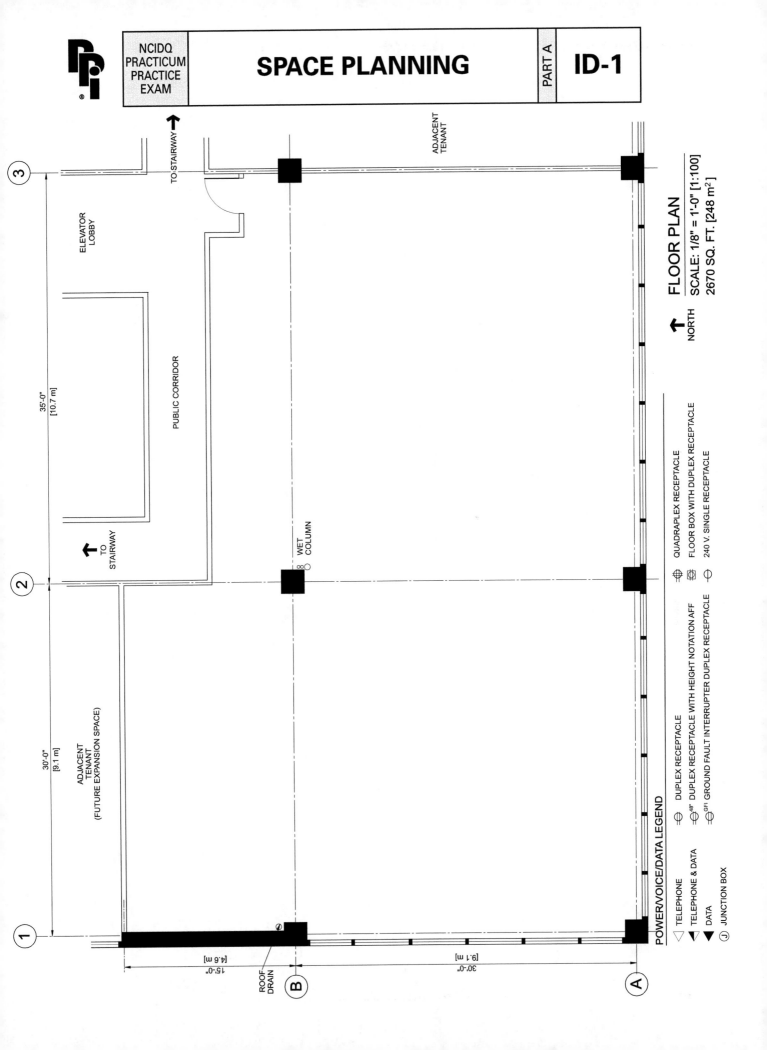

NCIDQ
PRACTICUM
PRACTICE
EXAM

SPACE PLANNING

PART A   **ID-1**

TO STAIRWAY

ADJACENT
TENANT

ELEVATOR
LOBBY

PUBLIC CORRIDOR

35'-0"
[10.7 m]

TO
STAIRWAY

WET
COLUMN

ADJACENT
TENANT
(FUTURE EXPANSION SPACE)

30'-0"
[9.1 m]

15'-0"
[4.6 m]

30'-0"
[9.1 m]

ROOF
DRAIN

FLOOR PLAN

NORTH

SCALE: 1/8" = 1'-0" [1:100]
2670 SQ. FT. [248 m²]

POWER/VOICE/DATA LEGEND

⊕ DUPLEX RECEPTACLE

⊕⁴⁸" DUPLEX RECEPTACLE WITH HEIGHT NOTATION AFF

⊕ᴳᶠᴵ GROUND FAULT INTERRUPTER DUPLEX RECEPTACLE

⊕ QUADRAPLEX RECEPTACLE

⊞ FLOOR BOX WITH DUPLEX RECEPTACLE

⊖ 240 V. SINGLE RECEPTACLE

▽ TELEPHONE

▼ TELEPHONE & DATA

▼ DATA

Ⓙ JUNCTION BOX

An exam-sized version of this worksheet can be downloaded from PPI's website at
www.ppi2pass.com/idpcpxdrawings.

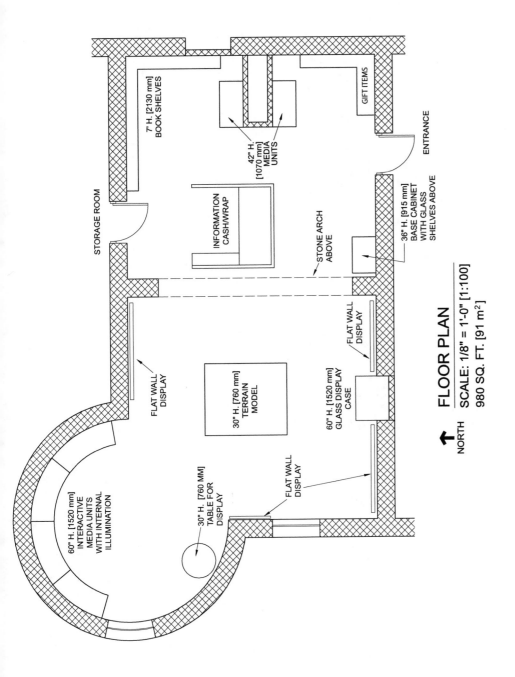

FLOOR PLAN

SCALE: 1/8" = 1'-0" [1:100]

980 SQ. FT. [91 m²]

NORTH

STORAGE ROOM

7' H. [2130 mm] BOOK SHELVES

42" H. [1070 mm] MEDIA UNITS

GIFT ITEMS

ENTRANCE

INFORMATION CASH/WRAP

STONE ARCH ABOVE

36" H. [915 mm] BASE CABINET WITH GLASS SHELVES ABOVE

FLAT WALL DISPLAY

FLAT WALL DISPLAY

30" H. [760 mm] TERRAIN MODEL

60" H. [1520 mm] GLASS DISPLAY CASE

FLAT WALL DISPLAY

60" H. [1520 mm] INTERACTIVE MEDIA UNITS WITH INTERNAL ILLUMINATION

30" H. [760 MM] TABLE FOR DISPLAY

An exam-sized version of this worksheet can be downloaded from PPI's website at
www.ppi2pass.com/idpcpxdrawings.

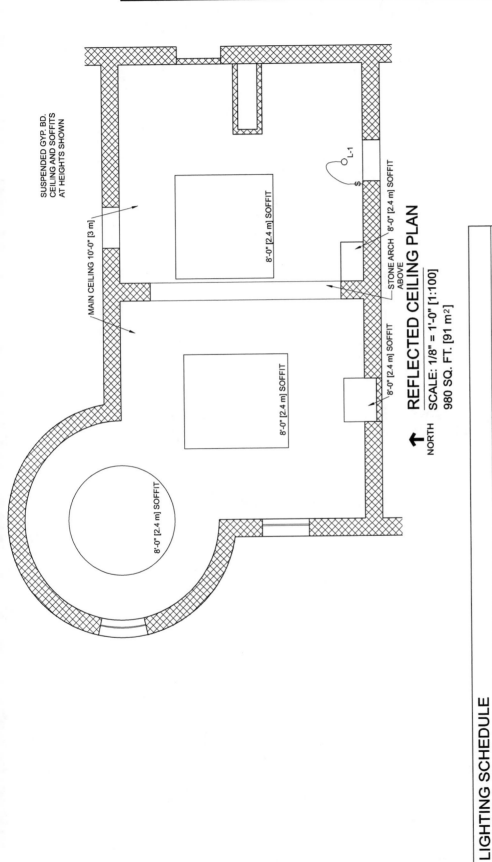

SUSPENDED GYP. BD. CEILING AND SOFFITS AT HEIGHTS SHOWN

MAIN CEILING 10'-0" [3 m]

8'-0" [2.4 m] SOFFIT

8'-0" [2.4 m] SOFFIT

8'-0" [2.4 m] SOFFIT

8'-0" [2.4 m] SOFFIT

STONE ARCH 8'-0" [2.4 m] SOFFIT ABOVE

L-1

REFLECTED CEILING PLAN

SCALE: 1/8" = 1'-0" [1:100]

980 SQ. FT. [91 m²]

NORTH

SWITCHING LEGEND

S	SINGLE POLE SWITCH
S_3	THREE-WAY SWITCH
S_D	DIMMER SWITCH
S_{DLV}	DIMMER SWITCH, LOW VOLTAGE
S_{OSS}	OCCUPANCY SENSOR/SWITCH COMBINATION
S_{DSS}	DAYLIGHT SENSOR/SWITCH COMBINATION

LIGHTING SCHEDULE

TAG	SYMBOL	WATTS/ FIXTURE	QUANTITY	TOTAL WATTS	NOTES AND SELECTION RATIONALE
L-1		32			CFL DOWNLIGHT
			TOTAL WATTS IN SOLUTION		
980 ft.² [91 m²]				DIVIDED BY SQ. FT. [m²] OF SPACE	
				= WATTS/SQ. FT. [m²]	

An exam-sized version of this worksheet can be downloaded from PPI's website at
www.ppi2pass.com/idpcpxdrawings.

PART B

INSTRUCTIONS

You will have two (2) hours in which to work the following three exercises.

- Exercise 3: Egress
- Exercise 4: Life Safety
- Exercise 5: Restroom (Washroom)

To complete these exercises, you will need

- Exercise Building Code Requirements
- Worksheet ID-3 (floor plan)
- Worksheet ID-4 (floor plan)
- Worksheet ID-5 (restroom/washroom plan)

For each exercise, you will be given a project description, project requirements, and required design instructions. Complete each solution on the appropriate worksheet. A thumbnail of the worksheet you will need is shown at the beginning of each exercise. As with the actual exam, reference materials are not permitted. Only this book's Exercise Building Code Requirements may be used.

If you finish Part B before the allotted time is up, check your solutions to make sure you've met all the project and building code requirements. On the actual exam, your solutions will be graded based on your ability to meet the required project and building code requirements, as well as your ability to demonstrate the level of knowledge and skill required to protect public health, safety, and welfare.

EXERCISE 3: EGRESS
PROJECT DESCRIPTION AND REQUIREMENTS

Project Description

The plan on worksheet ID-3 shows the upper story of a high-rise building with one fully planned tenant space. The building is classified as a business (B) occupancy, is constructed of protected steel construction with concrete floors, and is fully sprinklered.

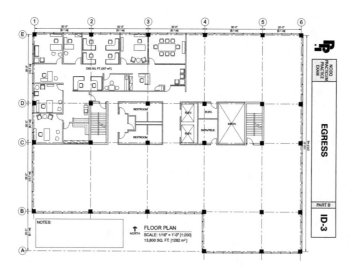

Project Requirements

Divide the remaining floor area into four (4) additional usable tenant suites with public circulation and egress spaces, to include the following.

- common egress corridor(s)
- one (1) 800 ft² (75 m²) minimum office suite
- one (1) 1900 ft² (177 m²) minimum office suite with southern exposure
- one (1) 2100 ft² (195 m²) minimum training area with tables and chairs
- one (1) 2800 ft² (260 m²) minimum office suite
- one (1) existing office suite (provided)

Required Design Solution

For this exercise, use information given on worksheet ID-3.

Instructions to Candidate

1. Subdivide space for a total of five (5) suites using the areas in square feet (square meters) listed in the project requirements.

    - Show demising walls and label actual area for each suite.
    - Calculate and label occupant load for each suite, using the occupancy load table in the building code requirements.

2. Create a common egress corridor.

   - Dimension egress corridor widths.
   - Show egress doors from all suites.
   - Draw barrier-free clearances at changes in direction along all egress routes.

3. Where two (2) means of egress are required in a suite, do the following.

   - Draw the proper method for determining door locations.
   - Dimension the distances required to show compliance with the building code requirements.

4. Draw and dimension the following.

   - the longest common path of travel for the existing suite
   - travel distance from the existing suite to the exit stairs

5. Calculate the occupant load per exit stair and indicate it in the area for notes. Assume equal distribution between stairs.

EXERCISE 4: LIFE SAFETY
PROJECT DESCRIPTION AND REQUIREMENTS

Project Description

The tenant space shown on worksheet ID-4 is a portion of the fifth floor of an eight-story office building. The space is occupied by an urban college and contains offices, a studio space, and a classroom. The building is constructed of a protected steel frame with concrete floors and curtain wall cladding, and it is fully sprinklered. The ceiling height of the entire floor is 9 ft 2 in (2.8 m).

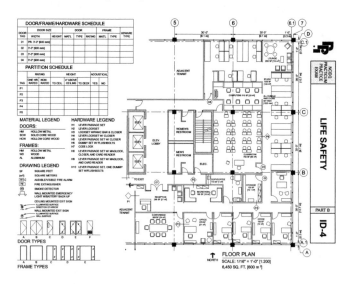

Project Requirements

Accommodate the following requirements.

- acoustic privacy for the conference room and the classroom
- card readers and associated hardware at each egress door of the suite
- secure and controlled access for storage room

Required Design Solution

For this exercise, use the information given on worksheet ID-4.

Instructions to Candidate

1. Complete the door/frame/hardware schedule for the doors tagged on the floor plan.

2. Complete the partition schedule for the partitions tagged on the floor plan.

3. Draw the following life safety equipment within the tenant suite, public corridors, public restrooms, and elevator lobby.

    - exit signs
    - smoke detectors
    - fire extinguishers
    - emergency lights with battery backup
    - audio/visual fire alarms

EXERCISE 5: RESTROOM (WASHROOM) PROJECT DESCRIPTION AND REQUIREMENTS

Project Description

Using all applicable code requirements, draw a layout of a men's restroom in the space given on the restroom (washroom) plan of worksheet ID-5.

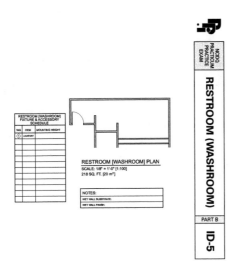

Project Requirements

Accommodate the following requirements.

- consideration of sight lines from the entrance into restroom so that fixtures, if seen from the entrance, are obscured by partitions
- plumbing fixtures located only on walls having a plumbing chase
- two (2) lavatories
- two (2) wall-hung toilets, including one (1) accessible toilet
- two (2) urinals, including one (1) accessible urinal
- grab bars as required by the Exercise Building Code Requirements
- accessible mirror
- accessible soap dispenser, 4 in wide × 12 in high × 4 in deep (100 mm wide × 300 mm high × 100 mm deep)
- accessible hand dryer, 12 in wide × 12 in high × 8 in deep (300 mm wide × 300 mm high × 200 mm deep)
- accessible trash receptacle

Required Design Solution

For this exercise, use the information given on worksheet ID-5.

Instructions to Candidate

1. Draw a plan view on the worksheet ID-5, and do the following.

    - Dimension centerlines of toilets and urinals.
    - Dimension stalls.
    - Dimension all grab bars.
    - Draw barrier-free clearances at accessible fixtures and changes in direction.

2. Graphically tag the following fixtures and accessories on worksheet ID-5.

    - lavatories
    - toilets
    - urinals
    - grab bars
    - soap dispenser
    - hand dryer
    - trash receptacle
    - mirror

3. Complete the fixture and accessory schedule on worksheet ID-5, and indicate the appropriate mounting heights for the following.

    - lavatories, counter height
    - toilets, seat
    - urinals, top of rim
    - grab bars, top of bar
    - soap dispenser, operable control
    - hand dryer, operable control
    - trash receptacle, opening
    - mirror, bottom edge

4. Complete the notes area on worksheet ID-5, and indicate the substrate and finish at the wet wall.

NCIDQ
PRACTICUM
PRACTICE
EXAM

EGRESS

PART B

ID-3

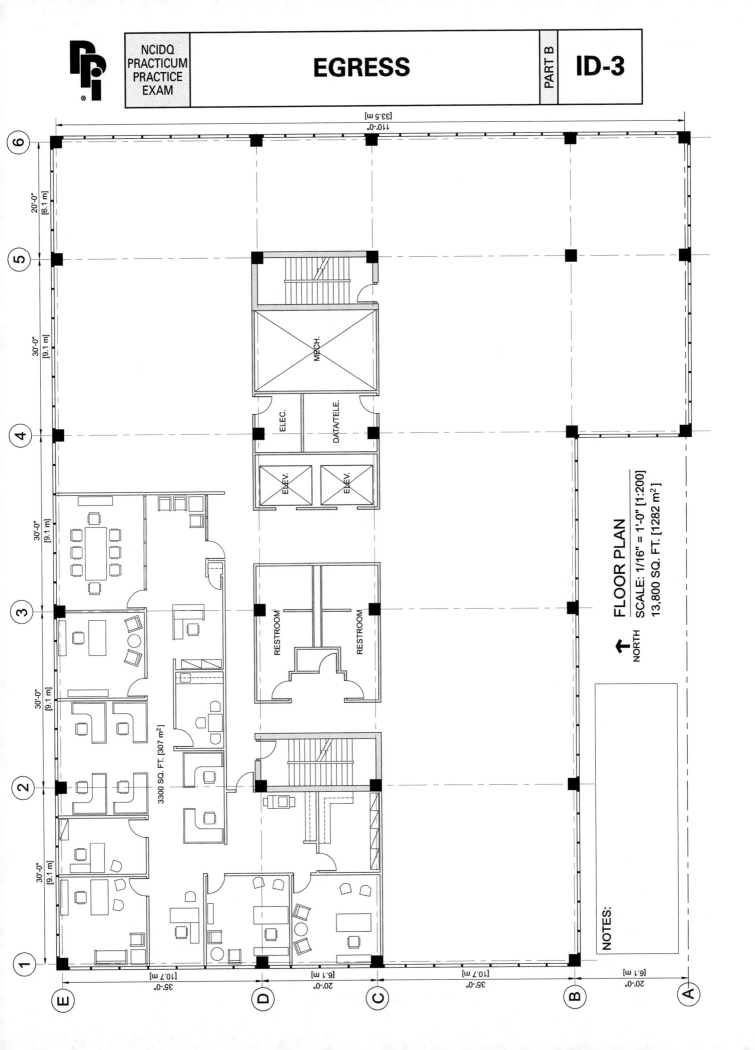

FLOOR PLAN
SCALE: 1/16" = 1'-0" [1:200]
13,800 SQ. FT. [1282 m²]

NORTH

NOTES:

3300 SQ. FT. [307 m²]

MECH.

ELEC.

DATA/TELE.

ELEV.

ELEV.

RESTROOM

RESTROOM

110'-0"
[33.5 m]

20'-0"
[6.1 m]

30'-0"
[9.1 m]

30'-0"
[9.1 m]

30'-0"
[9.1 m]

30'-0"
[9.1 m]

35'-0"
[10.7 m]

20'-0"
[6.1 m]

35'-0"
[10.7 m]

20'-0"
[6.1 m]

An exam-sized version of this worksheet can be downloaded from PPI's website at
www.ppi2pass.com/idpcpxdrawings.

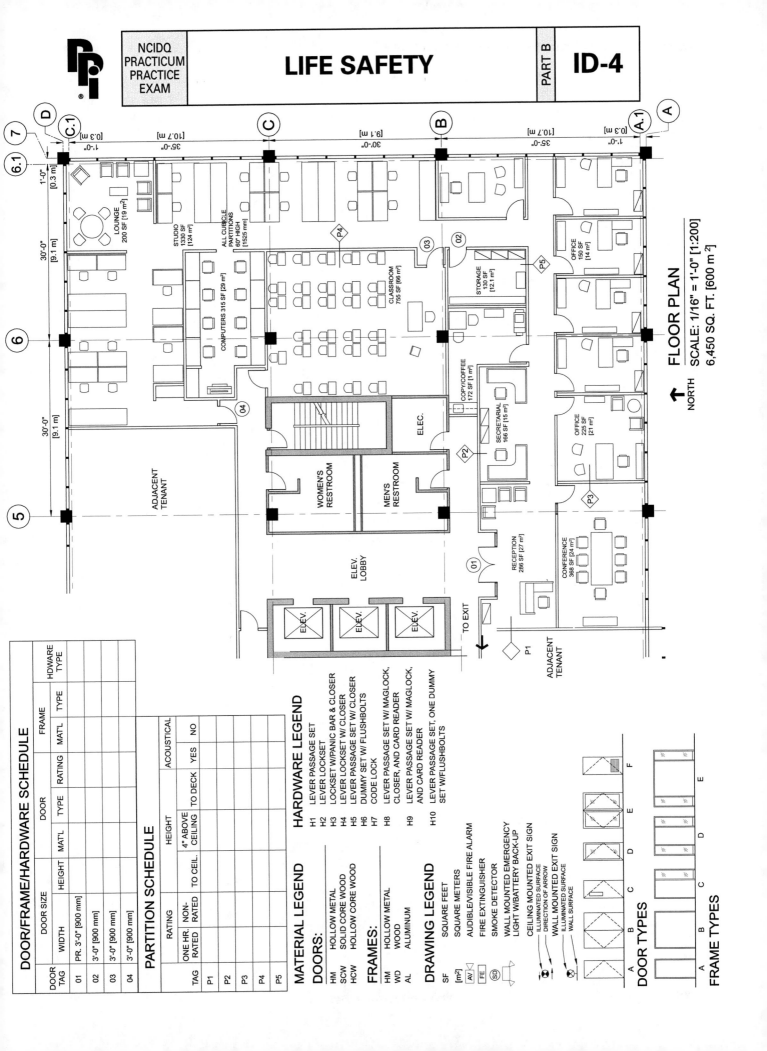

FLOOR PLAN

SCALE: 1/16" = 1'-0" [1:200]

6,450 SQ. FT. [600 m²]

NORTH

LOUNGE 200 SF [19 m²]

STUDIO 1330 SF [124 m²]

ALL CUBICLE PARTITIONS 60" HIGH [1525 mm]

COMPUTERS 315 SF [29 m²]

CLASSROOM 755 SF [86 m²]

STORAGE 130 SF [12.1 m²]

OFFICE 150 SF [14 m²]

COPY/COFFEE 172 SF [1 m²]

SECRETARIAL 166 SF [15 m²]

OFFICE 225 SF [21 m²]

ELEC.

WOMEN'S RESTROOM

MEN'S RESTROOM

ELEV. LOBBY

ELEV.

ELEV.

ELEV.

RECEPTION 286 SF [27 m²]

CONFERENCE 368 SF [24 m²]

TO EXIT

P1

ADJACENT TENANT

ADJACENT TENANT

P2 P3 P4 P5

01 02 03 04

DOOR/FRAME/HARDWARE SCHEDULE

DOOR TAG	DOOR SIZE			DOOR			FRAME			HDWARE TYPE
	WIDTH	HEIGHT	MAT'L	TYPE	RATING	MAT'L	TYPE			
01	PR. 3'-0" [900 mm]									
02	3'-0" [900 mm]									
03	3'-0" [900 mm]									
04	3'-0" [900 mm]									

PARTITION SCHEDULE

TAG	RATING		HEIGHT			ACOUSTICAL	
	ONE HR. RATED	NON-RATED	TO CEIL.	4" ABOVE CEILING	TO DECK	YES	NO
P1							
P2							
P3							
P4							
P5							

MATERIAL LEGEND

DOORS:
HM — HOLLOW METAL
SCW — SOLID CORE WOOD
HCW — HOLLOW CORE WOOD

FRAMES:
HM — HOLLOW METAL
WD — WOOD
AL — ALUMINUM

HARDWARE LEGEND

H1 — LEVER PASSAGE SET
H2 — LEVER LOCKSET
H3 — LOCKSET W/PANIC BAR & CLOSER
H4 — LEVER LOCKSET W/ CLOSER
H5 — LEVER PASSAGE SET W/ CLOSER
H6 — DUMMY SET W/ FLUSHBOLTS
H7 — CODE LOCK
H8 — LEVER PASSAGE SET W/ MAGLOCK, CLOSER, AND CARD READER
H9 — LEVER PASSAGE SET W/ MAGLOCK, AND CARD READER
H10 — LEVER PASSAGE SET, ONE DUMMY SET W/FLUSHBOLTS

DRAWING LEGEND

SF — SQUARE FEET
[m²] — SQUARE METERS
AV — AUDIBLE/VISIBLE FIRE ALARM
FE — FIRE EXTINGUISHER
SD — SMOKE DETECTOR
— WALL MOUNTED EMERGENCY LIGHT W/BATTERY BACK-UP
— CEILING MOUNTED EXIT SIGN
— ILLUMINATED SURFACE DIRECTION OF ARROW
— WALL MOUNTED EXIT SIGN
— ILLUMINATED SURFACE
— WALL SURFACE

DOOR TYPES
A B C D E F

FRAME TYPES
A B C D E

An exam-sized version of this worksheet can be downloaded from PPI's website at
www.ppi2pass.com/idpcpxdrawings.

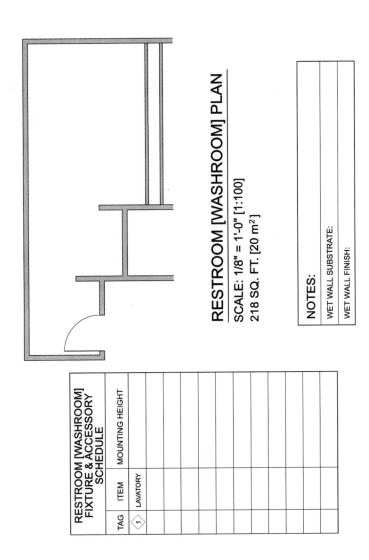

RESTROOM [WASHROOM] PLAN

SCALE: 1/8" = 1'-0" [1:100]
218 SQ. FT. [20 m²]

NOTES:

WET WALL SUBSTRATE:

WET WALL FINISH:

RESTROOM [WASHROOM] FIXTURE & ACCESSORY SCHEDULE

TAG	ITEM	MOUNTING HEIGHT
1	LAVATORY	

An exam-sized version of this worksheet can be downloaded from PPI's website at
www.ppi2pass.com/idpcpxdrawings.

PART C

INSTRUCTIONS

You will have two (2) hours in which to work the following two exercises.

- Exercise 6: Systems Integration

- Exercise 7: Millwork

To complete these exercises, you will need

- Exercise Building Code Requirements

- Worksheet ID-6a (reflected ceiling plan)

- Worksheet ID-6b (mechanical and sprinkler plan)

- Worksheet ID-7 (floor plan)

For each exercise, you will be given a project description, project requirements, and required design instructions. Complete each solution on the appropriate worksheet. Thumbnails of the worksheet or worksheets you will need are shown at the beginning of each exercise. As with the actual exam, reference materials are not permitted. Only this book's Exercise Building Code Requirements may be used.

If you finish Part C before the allotted time is up, check your solutions to make sure you've met all the project and building code requirements. On the actual exam, your solutions will be graded based on your ability to meet the required project and building code requirements, as well as your ability to demonstrate the level of knowledge and skill required to protect public health, safety, and welfare.

EXERCISE 6: SYSTEMS INTEGRATION
PROJECT DESCRIPTION AND REQUIREMENTS

Project Description

The plan shown on worksheet ID-6a is a tenant suite on the third floor of a six-story building. The ceiling is a combination of suspended gypsum wallboard and acoustical tile in a 24 in × 24 in (600 mm × 600 mm) grid. The space above the ceiling is a return air plenum and all walls extend to the structure above.

As engineers are often needed to design building systems, this exercise tests the ability to communicate design intent effectively in regard to areas where the various areas of professional practice interact.

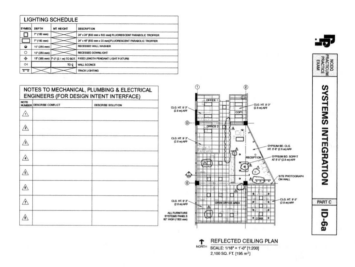

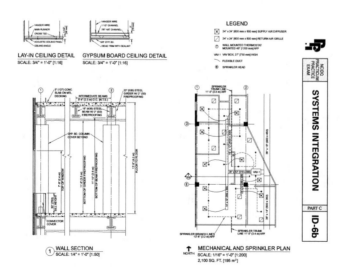

Project Requirements

1. Evaluate the plans provided for conflicts between furniture, lighting, mechanical, electrical, plumbing, and structural systems. Using the Exercise Building Code Requirements, complete the required design solution.

2. The following items MAY be relocated as needed.

    - light fixtures
    - electrical and mechanical controls
    - HVAC supply and return diffusers
    - sprinkler heads and sprinkler branch lines (lateral relocation only, not height)
    - gypsum board soffits and gypsum board clouds (height only)

3. The following items may NOT be changed or relocated.

    - quantity and size of elements shown
    - sprinkler trunk lines
    - HVAC air handling units and VAV boxes
    - HVAC trunk lines greater than 18 in (457 mm) wide
    - structural elements
    - furniture

Required Design Solution

For this exercise, use the information given on worksheets ID-6a and ID-6b.

Instructions to Candidate

1. On the reflected ceiling plan (worksheet ID-6a), draw and label the following.

    - 2 ft × 2 ft (600 mm × 600 mm) minimum access panel for the variable air volume box (VAV), where required (may be located immediately adjacent to the unit or underneath the unit where no ductwork is connected to the unit)

2. On the lighting schedule (worksheet ID-6a), indicate the following.

    - appropriate depth for the wall sconces shown in the reception area
    - appropriate mounting height AFF to the center line of wall sconces

3. On the reflected ceiling plan (worksheet ID-6a), eight (8) distinct objects are tagged, each tag indicating a coordination conflict. Referencing worksheets ID-6a and ID-6b, indicate solutions to these conflicts in the following ways.

    - On the notes schedule (worksheet ID-6a), write notes describing the conflicts and proposed solutions to be coordinated with mechanical, electrical, and plumbing engineers. Do this for each of the eight (8) tagged objects.
    - On the reflected ceiling plan (worksheet ID-6a), draw the new location for any objects recommended to be relocated. Each new location should resolve the coordination conflict and the drawing should express the design intent for the engineering consultants.

EXERCISE 7: MILLWORK
PROJECT DESCRIPTION AND REQUIREMENTS

Project Description

A small testing laboratory has decided to remodel a portion of its facility to make it more accessible. Most of the laboratory meets accessibility standards, but an island workstation must be redesigned to accommodate a wheelchair accessible sink and worksurface. As shown on worksheet ID-7, the area in which the work island is to be placed is in an alcove adjacent to the main laboratory area. The new work island must be placed in this area within the space defined by the change in flooring material.

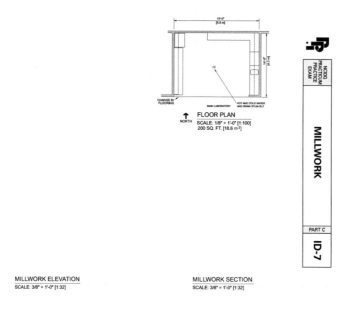

FLOOR PLAN
SCALE: 1/8" = 1'-0" [1:100]
200 SQ. FT. [18.6 m²]

MILLWORK ELEVATION
SCALE: 3/8" = 1'-0" [1:32]

MILLWORK SECTION
SCALE: 3/8" = 1'-0" [1:32]

Project Requirements

The requirements for the new workstation are the following.

- a minimum of 7 ft (2.1 m) of accessible work surface, including a small sink approximately 16 in (400 mm) wide, 16 in (400 mm) long, and 6 in (150 mm) deep. (See floor plan for the location of plumbing stub-outs.)

- a minimum of 7 ft (2.1 m) of standard height lab bench, 42 in (1067 mm) high

- two (2) accessible shelves under the standard height lab bench with a minimum depth of 2 ft (600 mm) and a minimum length of 3 ft (915 mm)

- closed storage cabinets below the standard height lab bench adjacent to the open shelving with a minimum depth of 2 ft (600 mm)

- a minimum of three (3) accessible duplex outlets

- countertop material appropriate for a laboratory

Required Design Solution

For this exercise, use worksheet ID-7.

Instructions to Candidate

1. Draw a plan view of the millwork solution on the floor plan.

    *   Indicate clearances for accessibility.
    *   Indicate the section cut and all elevations.
    *   Indicate the placement of the new sink to show an understanding of coordination needed between plumbing and millwork.
    *   Indicate three (3) accessible duplex outlets.

2. Draw one or more elevations of the millwork solution.

    *   Indicate and dimension accessible storage.
    *   Indicate and dimension accessible sink.
    *   Indicate dimensions for constructability.
    *   Indicate a minimum of two (2) appropriate finish materials, including one (1) countertop material.

3. Draw one (1) section that conveys the construction details at the accessible sink.

    *   Indicate dimensions for constructability.
    *   Indicate substrates.
    *   Indicate seaming or joinery to indicate limits of materials, if appropriate.

LIGHTING SCHEDULE

SYMBOL	DEPTH	MT. HEIGHT	DESCRIPTION
▭	7" (180 mm)		24" x 24" [600 mm x 600 mm] FLUORESCENT PARABOLIC TROFFER
▭	7" (180 mm)		24" x 48" [600 mm x 00 mm] FLUORESCENT PARABOLIC TROFFER
◑	10" (250 mm)		RECESSED WALL WASHER
○	10" (250 mm)		RECESSED DOWNLIGHT
◈	15" (380 mm)	7'-0" (2.1 m) TO BOT.	FIXED LENGTH PENDANT LIGHT FIXTURE
⊢○		TO ₵	WALL SCONCE
△△			TRACK LIGHTING

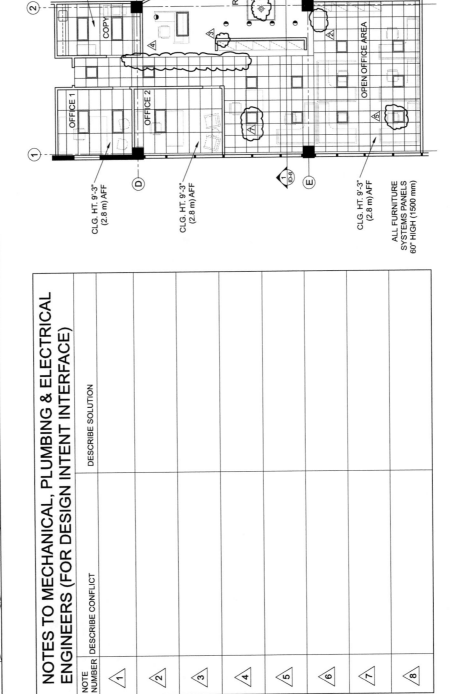

REFLECTED CEILING PLAN

SCALE: 1/16" = 1'-0" [1:200]
2,100 SQ. FT. [195 m²]

NORTH ↑

Labels on plan:
- CLG. HT. 9'-3" (2.8 m) AFF
- GYPSUM BD. CLG. HT. 8'-6" (2.6 m) AFF
- GYPSUM BD. SOFFIT AT 8'-0" (2.5 m) AFF
- SITE PHOTOGRAPH ON WALL
- COPY
- OFFICE 1
- OFFICE 2
- RECEPTION
- OPEN OFFICE AREA
- CONF.
- ALL FURNITURE SYSTEMS PANELS 60" HIGH (1500 mm)

NOTES TO MECHANICAL, PLUMBING & ELECTRICAL ENGINEERS (FOR DESIGN INTENT INTERFACE)

NOTE NUMBER	DESCRIBE CONFLICT	DESCRIBE SOLUTION
△1		
△2		
△3		
△4		
△5		
△6		
△7		
△8		

An exam-sized version of this worksheet can be downloaded from PPI's website at
www.ppi2pass.com/idpcpxdrawings.

LEGEND

⊠ 24" x 24" [600 mm x 600 mm] SUPPLY AIR DIFFUSER

⊡ 24" x 24" [600 mm x 600 mm] RETURN AIR GRILLE

Ⓣ WALL MOUNTED THERMOSTAT MOUNTED 48" [1200 mm] AFF

VAV-1 VAV BOX, 27" [750 mm] HIGH

╱ FLEXIBLE DUCT

⦿ SPRINKLER HEAD

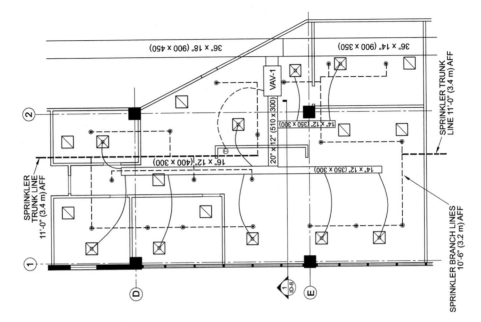

MECHANICAL AND SPRINKLER PLAN

↑ NORTH SCALE: 1/16" = 1'-0" [1:200]
2,100 SQ. FT. [195 m²]

Labels within plan:
- 36" x 18" (900 x 450)
- 36" x 14" (900 x 350)
- 14" x 12" (350 x 300)
- 20" x 12" (510 x 300) VAV-1
- 16" x 12" (400 x 300)
- 14" x 12" (350 x 300)
- SPRINKLER TRUNK LINE 11'-0" (3.4 m) AFF
- SPRINKLER BRANCH LINES 10'-6" (3.2 m) AFF
- ID-8
- ② ① Ⓓ Ⓔ

GYPSUM BOARD CEILING DETAIL

SCALE: 3/4" = 1'-0" [1:16]

- 3" [76 mm]
- HANGER WIRE
- 1 1/2" CHANNEL
- 7/8" HAT CHANNEL
- 5/8" GYP. BD.
- J BEAD TRIM WITH SEALANT

LAY-IN CEILING DETAIL

SCALE: 3/4" = 1'-0" [1:16]

- 1-1/2" [38 mm]
- HANGER WIRE
- MAIN RUNNER
- CROSS TEE
- ACOUSTIC CEILING PANEL
- CEILING ANGLE

WALL SECTION

① SCALE: 1/4" = 1'-0" [1:50]

- 20" (508) STEEL GIRDER W/ 2" (50) FIREPROOFING
- INTERMEDIATE BEAMS 8'-4" (2.5 m) O.C. (N.T.S.)
- 16" (406) STEEL BEAM W/ 2" (50) FIREPROOFING
- GYP. BD. COLUMN COVER BEYOND
- 5" (127) CONC. SLAB ON MTL. DECKING
- ②
- FLOOR TO FLOOR 13'-9" (4.2 m)
- BOTTOM OF BEAM FIREPROOFING 11'-10" (3.6 m)
- BOTTOM OF GIRDER FIREPROOFING 11'-6" (3.5 m)
- TOP OF WINDOW 7'-9" (2.4 m)
- SILL HEIGHT 30" (760)
- CONVECTOR COVER
- ①

An exam-sized version of this worksheet can be downloaded from PPI's website at
www.ppi2pass.com/idpcpxdrawings.

NCIDQ
PRACTICUM
PRACTICE
EXAM

MILLWORK

PART C **ID-7**

19'-0"
[5.8 m]

14'-0"
[4.3 m]

HOT AND COLD WATER
AND DRAIN STUB-OUT

MAIN LABORATORY

CHANGE IN
FLOORING

FLOOR PLAN

SCALE: 1/8" = 1'-0" [1:100]
200 SQ. FT. [18.6 m²]

NORTH

MILLWORK SECTION

SCALE: 3/8" = 1'-0" [1:32]

MILLWORK ELEVATION

SCALE: 3/8" = 1'-0" [1:32]

An exam-sized version of this worksheet can be downloaded from PPI's website at
www.ppi2pass.com/idpcpxdrawings.

PART A SOLUTIONS

EXERCISE 1: SPACE PLANNING

EXERCISE 2: LIGHTING DESIGN

EXERCISE 1: SPACE PLANNING
PASSING SOLUTION

This solution is planned well with the correct means of egress, almost all furniture and equipment included, and all items labeled as required. The following items are incorrect, but are minor enough to not cause this solution to fail.

1. The work/copy room, reception area, and coffee/lounge are all slightly under the minimum area requirements, but the planning shows that they would work in the manner planned. The shortage in area is less than 10% of the program requirements, which is normally acceptable. The east wall of the coffee/lounge could have been moved slightly to the east without affecting the planning of the reception area. The clerk's area is slightly oversized but meets the minimum requirements and shows a functional layout.

2. The printer/fax is missing from the receptionist's work area.

3. The outlet in the work room is labeled as 240 V, but uses the incorrect symbol for a 240 V outlet.

4. The trash receptacle in the men's restroom is too close to the door. This could have been drawn as the receptacle in the women's room was drawn.

PPi ®

TO STAIRWAY

ELEVATOR LOBBY

PUBLIC CORRIDOR

TO STAIRWAY

35'-0" [10.7 m]

30'-0" [9.1 m]

ADJACENT TENANT

ADJACENT TENANT (FUTURE EXPANSION SPACE)

2ND EXIT

EXPANSION

WORK ROOM 140 S.F.

BINDING

CLERK 130 S.F.

ASST. DEAN 150 S.F.

DEAN 225 S.F.

FILE ROOM 123 S.F.

COFFEE/LOUNGE 152 S.F.

REF
MICRO WAVE
COFFEE
SINK
WET COLUMN

RECEPTION 330 S.F.

LIT. RACK

ACCESSIBLE COUNTER

FILES UNDER COUNTER

TELE. 20 S.F.

SERVER

60"

WOMEN 64 S.F.
DRYER
SOAP
MIRROR
TRASH

MEN 64 S.F.
96" GRAB BAR
30"×48"

54"

54"

CONFERENCE 298 S.F.

CLOS. 10 S.F.

ADVISING 150 S.F.

ADVISING 150 S.F.
PHONE
PC

SECRETARY 150 S.F.

FILE

PC
PHONE

3'×4'6"

240 V.

42"
42"

ROOF DRAIN

B

15'-0" [4.6 m]

30'-0" [9.1 m]

1   2   3

1

A

FLOOR PLAN

NORTH

SCALE: 1/8" = 1'-0" [1:100]
2670 SQ. FT. [248 m²]

POWER/VOICE/DATA LEGEND

▽ TELEPHONE
▼ TELEPHONE & DATA
▼ DATA
Ⓙ JUNCTION BOX

⊕ DUPLEX RECEPTACLE
⊕48" DUPLEX RECEPTACLE WITH HEIGHT NOTATION AFF
⊕GFI GROUND FAULT INTERRUPTER DUPLEX RECEPTACLE

⊕ QUADRAPLEX RECEPTACLE
⊞ FLOOR BOX WITH DUPLEX RECEPTACLE
⊕ 240 V. SINGLE RECEPTACLE

EXERCISE 1: SPACE PLANNING
FAILING SOLUTION

The following errors are significant enough to contribute to the failure of this solution.

1. The most serious error is the dead-end corridor, which exceeds the maximum allowable length of 20 ft (6 m).

2. Related to the dead-end corridor is the lack of any provision for expansion as required by the program. If the file room were changed to allow for expansion to the north, there would not be enough space for the files.

3. There is only 12 in (300 mm) maneuvering clearance on the pull side of the door to the coffee/lounge. 18 in (450 mm) is required.

4. There is less than 18 in (450 mm) on the pull side of the door into the assistant dean's office. This could have been easily corrected by drawing the furniture farther away from the door.

5. No grab bars are shown in the restrooms.

6. The work/copy room is too large by a significant amount (more than 15%) and there is an unnecessary table indicated.

7. The binding machine required in the work room is not indicated.

8   Although the clerk and secretarial spaces function, the layout is awkward and the file cabinets required for each area share the same space.

9. There is only one file in the advising area when two are required.

10. Although a note indicates that the same layout is to be used in both advising offices, the furniture and equipment should have been drawn in both rooms.

11. The outlets above the countertop in the coffee/lounge are not marked for height above finish floor (AFF).

12. A convenience outlet is needed on each of the south and east walls of the coffee/lounge.

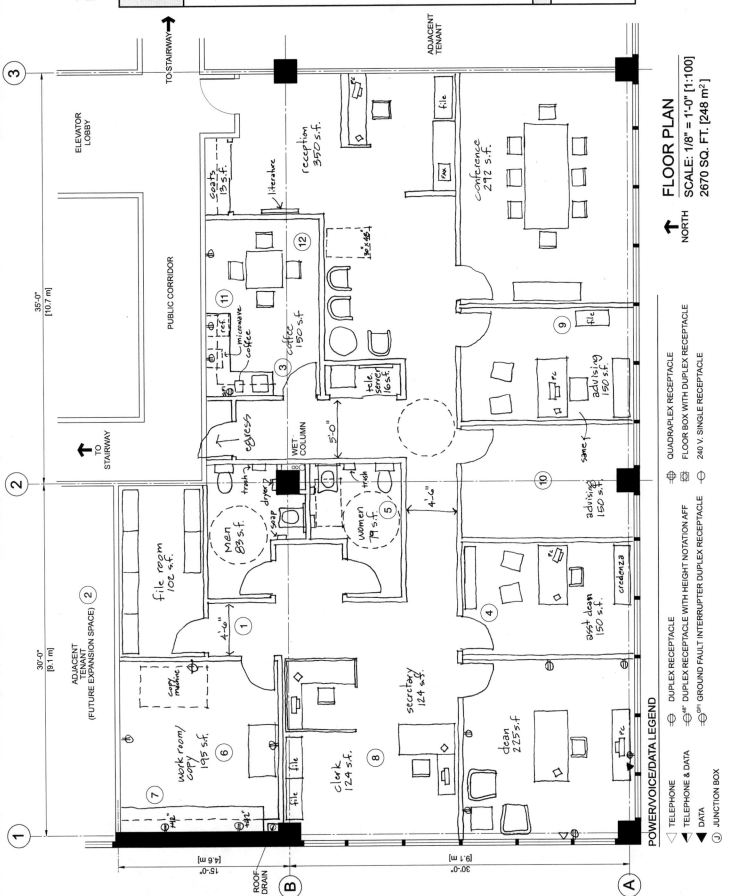

FLOOR PLAN
SCALE: 1/8" = 1'-0" [1:100]
2670 SQ. FT. [248 m²]

NORTH

POWER/VOICE/DATA LEGEND

TELEPHONE ▽ — DUPLEX RECEPTACLE ⊕ — QUADRAPLEX RECEPTACLE

TELEPHONE & DATA ▼ — ⊕⁴⁸" DUPLEX RECEPTACLE WITH HEIGHT NOTATION AFF — ⊞ FLOOR BOX WITH DUPLEX RECEPTACLE

DATA ▼ — ⊕ᴳᶠᴵ GROUND FAULT INTERRUPTER DUPLEX RECEPTACLE — ⊖ 240 V. SINGLE RECEPTACLE

ⱼ JUNCTION BOX

EXERCISE 2: LIGHTING DESIGN
PASSING SOLUTION

This solution uses appropriate luminaires for the various lighting tasks. Low-wattage fixtures are selected and the lighting budget is not exceeded.

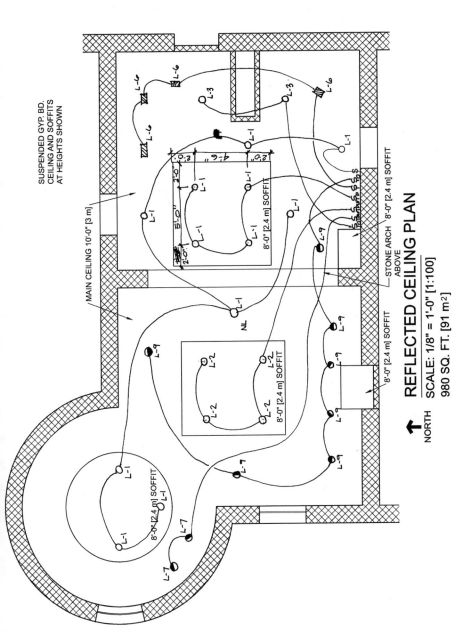

SUSPENDED GYP. BD. CEILING AND SOFFITS AT HEIGHTS SHOWN

MAIN CEILING 10'-0" [3 m]

L-3

L-3

L-1

L-1

L-1

L-1

L-1

L-1

L-1

L-1

2'-0"   4'-6"   2'-0"

5'-0"

2'-0"

8'-0" [2.4 m] SOFFIT

8'-0" [2.4 m] SOFFIT

STONE ARCH 8'-0" [2.4 m] SOFFIT ABOVE

L-9

S S S_D S_{DSS}

L-1

NL

L-9

L-9

L-2

L-2

L-2

L-2

L-2

8'-0" [2.4 m] SOFFIT

L-9

L-9

L-7

L-1

L-1

8'-0" [2.4 m] SOFFIT

L-1

L-7

L-7

REFLECTED CEILING PLAN

SCALE: 1/8" = 1'-0" [1:100]
980 SQ. FT. [91 m²]

NORTH

SWITCHING LEGEND

S SINGLE POLE SWITCH

S_3 THREE-WAY SWITCH

S_D DIMMER SWITCH

S_{DLV} DIMMER SWITCH, LOW VOLTAGE

S_{OSS} OCCUPANCY SENSOR/SWITCH COMBINATION

S_{DSS} DAYLIGHT SENSOR/SWITCH COMBINATION

LIGHTING SCHEDULE

TAG	SYMBOL	WATTS/ FIXTURE	QUANTITY	TOTAL WATTS	NOTES AND SELECTION RATIONALE
L-1	○	32	12	384	CFL DOWNLIGHT – General ambient light with low wattage
L-2	○	75	4	300	Good spread control; sparkle; white light on model
L-3	○	24	2	48	Low wattage; general illumination on media units
L-6	▨	54	4	216	Broad illumination on shelving
L-7	◗	75	2	150	Spot highlight on display table; MR-16 provides range of spread options
L-9	◗	32	7	224	Wallwash on vertical display panels and case with low voltage
					TOTAL WATTS IN SOLUTION
				1,322	
				980 ft²[91 m²]	DIVIDED BY SQ. FT. [m²] OF SPACE
				1.35	= WATTS/SQ. FT. [m²]

EXERCISE 2: LIGHTING DESIGN
FAILING SOLUTION

The following errors are significant enough to contribute to the failure of this solution.

1. The lighting allowance is exceeded by a significant amount. This is due in part to using luminaires with excessive wattages, but also due to the overlighting of the space.

2. Wall washers are not appropriate for the internally illuminated media units.

3. Wall washers are not appropriate for the two media units in the east portion of the space.

4. The sconces are not ADA compliant as they are more than 4 in (102 mm) deep and are mounted 72 in (1830 mm) above the floor.

5. The wall sconce near the entry is not switched.

6. Ambient and task lighting are not switched separately as required.

7. Fixtures L-1 and L-5 are switched together even though they are different lamp types.

8. Fixtures L-8 and L-16 are switched together even though they are different lamp types.

9. Fixtures L-4 and L-12 are switched together even though they are different lamp types.

10. Dimensions are missing from the luminaires over the cash/wrap station.

11. Fixture L-9 is overused on the bookshelves.

12. No indication is given as to which fixture is a night security light.

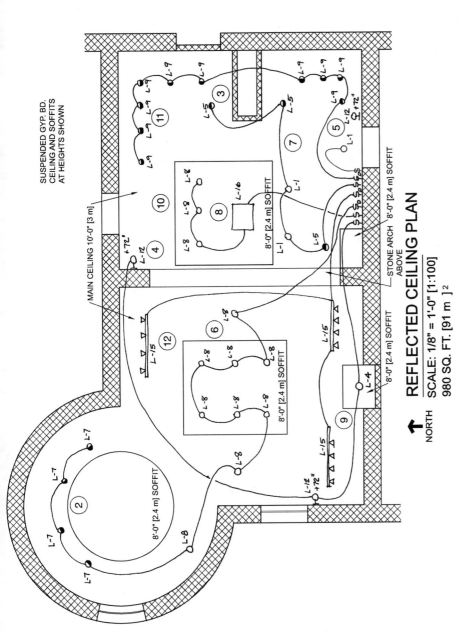

SUSPENDED GYP. BD. CEILING AND SOFFITS AT HEIGHTS SHOWN

MAIN CEILING 10'-0" [3 m]

8'-0" [2.4 m] SOFFIT

8'-0" [2.4 m] SOFFIT

8'-0" [2.4 m] SOFFIT

8'-0" [2.4 m] SOFFIT

STONE ARCH ABOVE

8'-0" [2.4 m] SOFFIT

REFLECTED CEILING PLAN
SCALE: 1/8" = 1'-0" [1:100]
980 SQ. FT. [91 m]²

NORTH

SWITCHING LEGEND

S	SINGLE POLE SWITCH
S_3	THREE-WAY SWITCH
S_D	DIMMER SWITCH
S_{DLV}	DIMMER SWITCH, LOW VOLTAGE
S_{OSS}	OCCUPANCY SENSOR/SWITCH COMBINATION
S_{DSS}	DAYLIGHT SENSOR/SWITCH COMBINATION

LIGHTING SCHEDULE

TAG	SYMBOL	WATTS/ FIXTURE	QUANTITY	TOTAL WATTS	NOTES AND SELECTION RATIONALE
L-1	○	32	3	96	CFL DOWNLIGHT – GENERAL LIGHTING
L-4	○	150	1	150	BRIGHT HIGHLIGHT OF CASE
L-5	◑	78	3	234	WALL WASH OF DISPLAY AND MEDIA
L-7	○	75	4	300	HIGHLIGHT MEDIA UNITS
L-8	◑	100	12	1200	TASK LIGHTING AND GENERAL AMBIENT
L-9	◕	32	10	320	HIGHLIGHT BOOKSHELVES
L-12	⬚	35	3	105	AMBIENT LIGHT
L-15	▱	240	3	720	DRAMATIC HIGHLIGHT OF WALL DISPLAYS
L-16	☐	64	1	64	TASK LIGHT OVER WORK COUNTER
				3189	TOTAL WATTS IN SOLUTION
				980 ft² [91 m²]	DIVIDED BY SQ. FT. [m²] OF SPACE
				3.25	= WATTS/SQ. FT. [m²]

PART B SOLUTIONS

EXERCISE 3: EGRESS

EXERCISE 4: LIFE SAFETY

EXERCISE 5: RESTROOM (WASHROOM)

EXERCISE 3: EGRESS
PASSING SOLUTION

This solution includes all the required notations and has the four tenant spaces properly planned. The training area has an awkward space at the southeast portion, but is difficult to avoid given the base building layout. The awkward space alone would not cause this solution to fail.

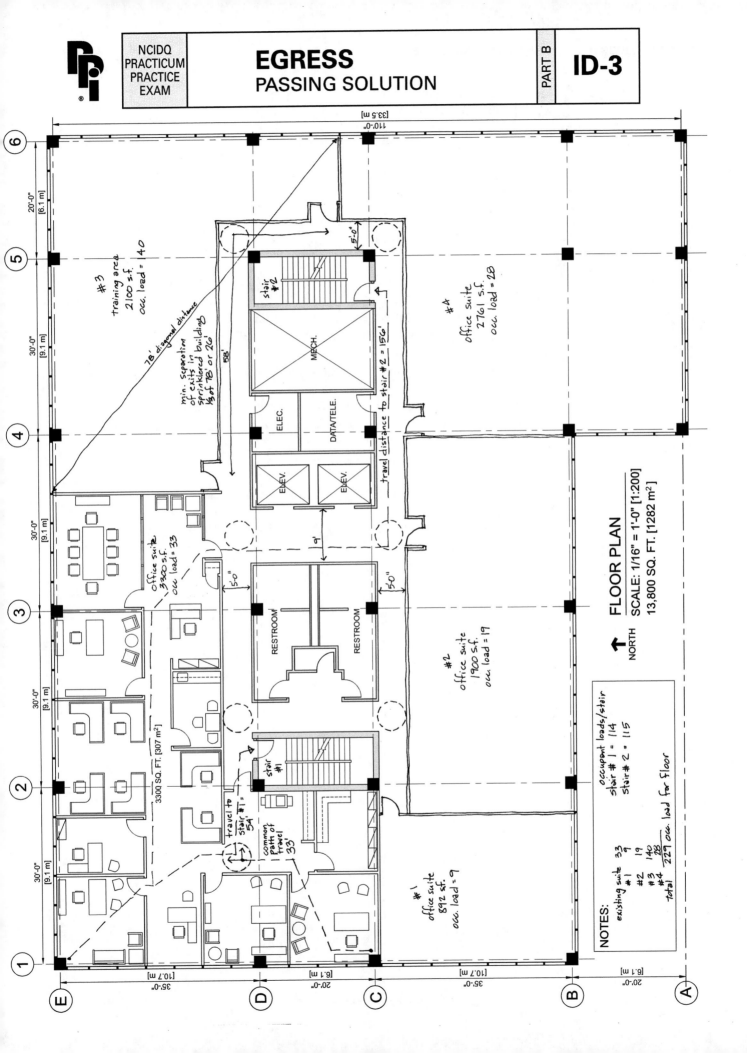

FLOOR PLAN
SCALE: 1/16" = 1'-0" [1:200]
13,800 SQ. FT. [1282 m²]

NORTH

#3
training area
2100 s.f.
occ. load = 40

min. separation
of exits in
sprinkled building
1/3 of 78' or 26'

78' diagonal distance

58'

stair #2

MECH.

ELEC.

DATA/TELE.

ELEV.

ELEV.

#4
office suite
2761 s.f.
occ. load = 28

travel distance to stair #2 = 156'

5'-0"

office suite
3300 s.f.
occ. load = 33

3300 SQ. FT. [307 m²]

5'-0"

9'

RESTROOM

RESTROOM

5'-0"

#2
office suite
1900 s.f.
occ. load = 19

stair #1

travel to
stair #1 =
54'

common
path of
travel
33'

#1
office suite
892 s.f.
occ. load = 9

NOTES:

existing suite
#1   33
#2   19
#3   140
#4   28
Total 229 occ. load for floor

occupant loads/stair
stair #1 = 114
stair #2 = 115

EXERCISE 3: EGRESS
FAILING SOLUTION

The following errors are significant enough to contribute to the failure of this solution.

1. The corridor to the entrance of the large office suite exceeds the dead-end corridor limit of 20 ft (6 m).

2. The size of the large office suite exceeds the project requirements of 2800 ft² (260 m²) by more than 10%, which should generally be avoided.

3. The length of the travel distance is incorrectly calculated from the end of the common path of egress travel instead of from the farthest point in the suite. Also, this is not the longest common path of egress travel in the suite; the path from the southwest corner of the suite is the longest and should be labeled and dimensioned.

4. Widths should be shown for all egress paths, including the width of the elevator lobby.

5. The diagonal distance of the training area is incorrectly calculated using the shortest diagonal distance instead of the greatest distance.

6. The smaller office suite is undersized.

7. The layout of the 1900 ft² (177 m²) office suite is awkward.

8. Barrier-free access clearances should be shown as 5 ft (1.5 m) dashed circles at all changes of direction.

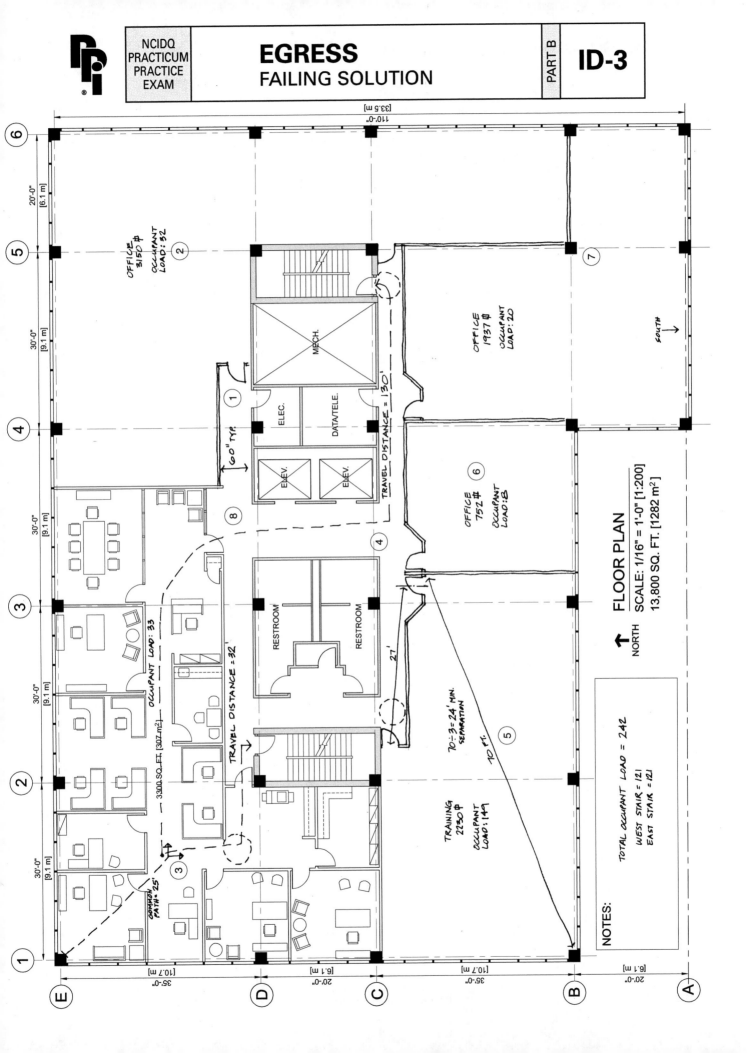

FLOOR PLAN

SCALE: 1/16" = 1'-0" [1:200]

13,800 SQ. FT. [1282 m²]

NORTH

OFFICE 3150 # OCCUPANT LOAD: 52

OFFICE 1937 # OCCUPANT LOAD: 20

OFFICE 752 # OCCUPANT LOAD: 8

MECH.

ELEC.

DATA/TELE.

ELEV.

ELEV.

TRAVEL DISTANCE = 130'

60" TYP.

RESTROOM

RESTROOM

TRAVEL DISTANCE = 32'

OCCUPANT LOAD: 33

3300 SQ. FT. [307 m²]

COMMON PATH = 25'

TRAINING 2150 # OCCUPANT LOAD: 144

10÷3 = 24' MIN. SEPARATION

27'

70 FT.

SOUTH

NOTES:

TOTAL OCCUPANT LOAD = 242

WEST STAIR = 121

EAST STAIR = 121

EXERCISE 4: LIFE SAFETY
PASSING SOLUTION

This solution shows a good overall understanding of the program requirements. It has only the following minor errors, which are not significant enough to cause it to fail.

1. There should be a ceiling-mounted exit light in the public corridor outside the main entry door to the suite.

2. A smoke detector is missing in the computer room.

3. There are only two fire extinguishers in the suite. Both are within 75 ft (23 m) of all occupants, but the Exercise Building Code Requirements requires one for every 3000 ft² (280 m²). Because the suite is over 6000 ft², there must be three.

4. Door #01 and its frame should be type E, based on the plan drawing showing glazing on both sides of the door.

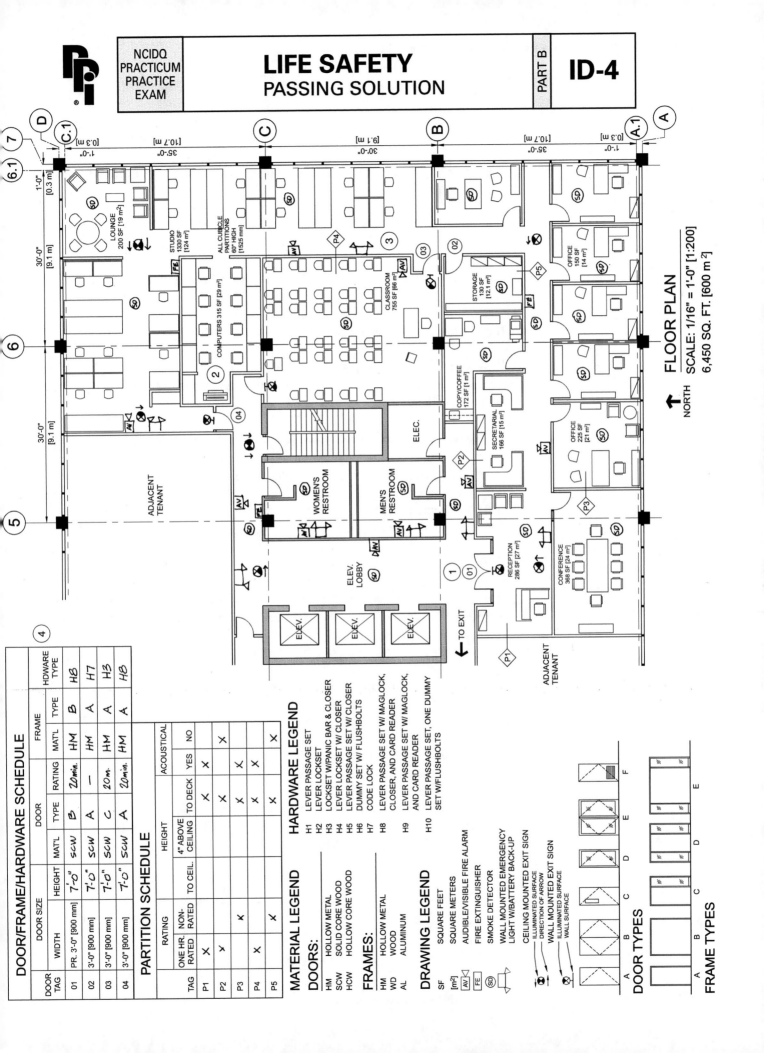

FLOOR PLAN

NORTH SCALE: 1/16" = 1'-0" [1:200]
6,450 SQ. FT. [600 m²]

DOOR/FRAME/HARDWARE SCHEDULE

DOOR TAG	DOOR SIZE WIDTH	DOOR HEIGHT	DOOR MAT'L	DOOR TYPE	FRAME RATING	FRAME MAT'L	FRAME TYPE	HDWARE TYPE
01	PR. 3'-0" [900 mm]	7'-0"	SCW	B	20min.	HM	B	H8
02	3'-0" [900 mm]	7'-0"	SCW	A	–	HM	A	H7
03	3'-0" [900 mm]	7'-0"	SCW	C	20m.	HM	A	H3
04	3'-0" [900 mm]	7'-0"	SCW	A	20min.	HM	A	H8

PARTITION SCHEDULE

TAG	RATING ONE HR. RATED	RATING NON-RATED	HEIGHT TO CEIL.	HEIGHT 4" ABOVE CEILING	HEIGHT TO DECK	ACOUSTICAL YES	ACOUSTICAL NO
P1	X				X	X	
P2		X		X	X		X
P3		X			X	X	
P4	X				X	X	
P5		X			X		X

MATERIAL LEGEND

DOORS:
HM HOLLOW METAL
SCW SOLID CORE WOOD
HCW HOLLOW CORE WOOD

FRAMES:
HM HOLLOW METAL
WD WOOD
AL ALUMINUM

HARDWARE LEGEND

H1 LEVER PASSAGE SET
H2 LEVER LOCKSET
H3 LOCKSET W/PANIC BAR & CLOSER
H4 LEVER LOCKSET W/ CLOSER
H5 LEVER PASSAGE SET W/ CLOSER
H6 DUMMY SET W/ FLUSHBOLTS
H7 CODE LOCK
H8 LEVER PASSAGE SET W/ MAGLOCK, CLOSER, AND CARD READER
H9 LEVER PASSAGE SET W/ MAGLOCK, AND CARD READER
H10 LEVER PASSAGE SET, ONE DUMMY SET W/FLUSHBOLTS

DRAWING LEGEND

SF SQUARE FEET
[m²] SQUARE METERS
AV AUDIBLE/VISIBLE FIRE ALARM
FE FIRE EXTINGUISHER
SD SMOKE DETECTOR
WALL MOUNTED EMERGENCY LIGHT W/BATTERY BACK-UP
CEILING MOUNTED EXIT SIGN
ILLUMINATED SURFACE
DIRECTION OF ARROW
WALL MOUNTED EXIT SIGN
ILLUMINATED SURFACE
WALL SURFACE

DOOR TYPES
A B C D E F

FRAME TYPES
A B C D E F

Floor plan room labels
LOUNGE 200 SF [19 m²]
STUDIO 1330 SF [124 m²]
ALL CUBICLE PARTITIONS 60" HIGH [1525 mm]
COMPUTERS 315 SF [29 m²]
CLASSROOM 755 SF [66 m²]
STORAGE 130 SF [12.1 m²]
OFFICE 150 SF [14 m²]
COPY/COFFEE 172 SF [1 m²]
SECRETARIAL 166 SF [15 m²]
OFFICE 225 SF [21 m²]
ELEC.
WOMEN'S RESTROOM
MEN'S RESTROOM
ELEV. LOBBY
RECEPTION 286 SF [27 m²]
CONFERENCE 368 SF [24 m²]
ADJACENT TENANT
ELEV.
TO EXIT

EXERCISE 4: LIFE SAFETY
FAILING SOLUTION

The following errors are significant enough to contribute to the failure of this solution.

1.   The exit sign at the stairway should be a ceiling-mounted unit with arrows pointing in the direction of the door.

2.   The exit sign in the elevator lobby shows incorrect illuminated sides and has no arrow indication.

3.   Exit signs in the suite have no arrow indications and are illuminated on the wrong sides.

4.   The public corridors lack life safety equipment.

5.   There are only two fire extinguishers in the suite. Both are within 75 ft (23 m) of all occupants, but the Exercise Building Code Requirements require one for every 3000 ft^2 (280 m^2). Because the suite is over 6000 ft^2, there must be three.

6.   The Exercise Building Code Requirements do not require an emergency light in the classroom. One unnecessary emergency light is a minor error and would not by itself cause a solution to fail, but a greater number of unnecessary lights could.

7.   There are no emergency lights in the restrooms and one of the public corridors, though they are required by the Exercise Building Code Requirements.

8.   There are no audio/visual alarms in the classroom and public corridors.

9.   Door #01 must be 20-minute rated, and the glass doors are not appropriate. The hardware should be type H8 with closers and card readers as required by the program.

10. Door #02 must be a minimum of 7 ft (2 m) high as required by the program.

11. A full glass door is not appropriate for door #03.

12. Door #04 should have hardware with a card reader and closer, such as type H8.

13. The partition between the conference room and the adjacent office should extend to the deck for acoustic privacy as required by the program.

14. The partition between the classroom and the corridor should extend to the deck and be indicated as an acoustical partition for acoustic privacy as required by the project. The partition must be 1-hour rated as stated in the code requirements.

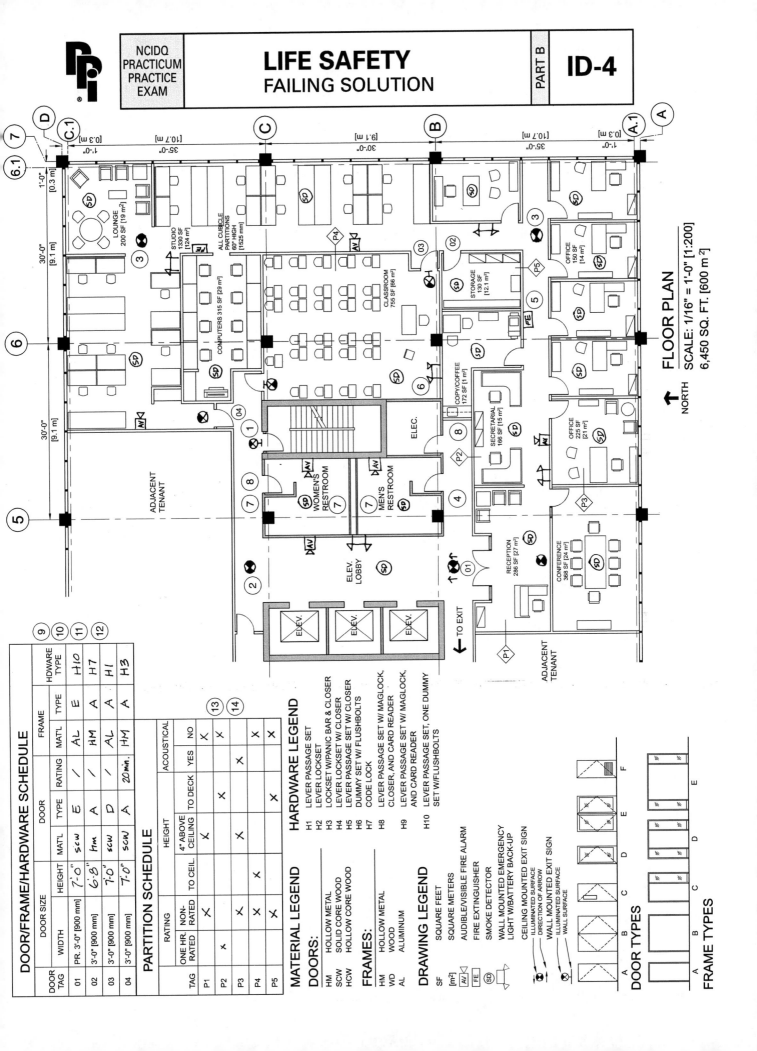

FLOOR PLAN
SCALE: 1/16" = 1'-0" [1:200]
6,450 SQ. FT. [600 m²]
NORTH

DOOR/FRAME/HARDWARE SCHEDULE

DOOR TAG	DOOR SIZE WIDTH	HEIGHT	DOOR MAT'L	DOOR TYPE	RATING	FRAME MAT'L	FRAME TYPE	HDWARE TYPE
01	PR. 3'-0" [900 mm]	7'-0"	SCW	E	/	AL	E	H10
02	3'-0" [900 mm]	6'-8"	HM	A	/	HM	A	H7
03	3'-0" [900 mm]	7'-0"	SCW	D	/	AL	A	H1
04	3'-0" [900 mm]	7'-0"	SCW	A	20 min.	HM	A	H3

| | 9 | 10 | 11 | 12 |

PARTITION SCHEDULE

TAG	RATING ONE HR. RATED	RATING NON-RATED	HEIGHT TO CEIL.	HEIGHT 4" ABOVE CEILING	HEIGHT TO DECK	ACOUSTICAL YES	ACOUSTICAL NO
P1		X	X				X
P2	X			X	X		X
P3		X	X			X	
P4	X						X
P5	X				X		X

| | | | | | | 13 | 14 |

MATERIAL LEGEND

DOORS:
HM   HOLLOW METAL
SCW   SOLID CORE WOOD
HCW   HOLLOW CORE WOOD

FRAMES:
HM   HOLLOW METAL
WD   WOOD
AL   ALUMINUM

HARDWARE LEGEND

H1   LEVER PASSAGE SET
H2   LEVER LOCKSET
H3   LOCKSET W/PANIC BAR & CLOSER
H4   LEVER LOCKSET W/ CLOSER
H5   LEVER PASSAGE SET W/ CLOSER
H6   DUMMY SET W/ FLUSHBOLTS
H7   CODE LOCK
H8   LEVER PASSAGE SET W/ MAGLOCK, CLOSER, AND CARD READER
H9   LEVER PASSAGE SET W/ MAGLOCK, AND CARD READER
H10   LEVER PASSAGE SET, ONE DUMMY SET W/FLUSHBOLTS

DRAWING LEGEND

SF   SQUARE FEET
[m²]   SQUARE METERS
AV   AUDIBLE/VISIBLE FIRE ALARM
FE   FIRE EXTINGUISHER
SD   SMOKE DETECTOR
WALL MOUNTED EMERGENCY LIGHT W/BATTERY BACK-UP
CEILING MOUNTED EXIT SIGN
ILLUMINATED SURFACE
DIRECTION OF ARROW
WALL MOUNTED EXIT SIGN
ILLUMINATED SURFACE
WALL SURFACE

DOOR TYPES

A   B   C   D   E   F

FRAME TYPES

A   B   C   D   E   F

EXERCISE 5: RESTROOM (WASHROOM)
PASSING SOLUTION

This solution meets nearly all the program requirements. Though the length of the standard toilet stall is not dimensioned and the second soap dispenser is not tagged, these are minor errors not significant enough to cause the solution to fail.

NCIDQ
PRACTICUM
PRACTICE
EXAM

RESTROOM (WASHROOM)
PASSING SOLUTION

PART C

ID-5

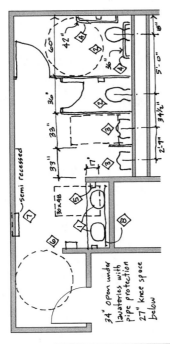

semi recessed

30x48

34" open under
lavatories with
pipe protection
27" knee space
below

RESTROOM [WASHROOM] PLAN

SCALE: 1/8" = 1'-0" [1:100]
218 SQ. FT. [20 m²]

NOTES:

WET WALL SUBSTRATE: _cementitious backer board_

WET WALL FINISH: _ceramic tile_

RESTROOM [WASHROOM] FIXTURE & ACCESSORY SCHEDULE		
TAG	ITEM	MOUNTING HEIGHT
1	LAVATORY	34" AFF
2	Toilets	18" AFF
3	urinal	17" to rim
4	grab bars	34" AFF
5	soap dispenser	40" AFF to controls
6	hand dryer	40" AFF to controls
7	trash	40" AFF–4" max. projection
8	mirror	bottom 4'-0" AFF

EXERCISE 5: RESTROOM (WASHROOM)
FAILING SOLUTION

The following errors are significant enough to contribute to the failure of this solution.

1. Barrier-free clearance is shown at the lavatory, but it does not extend 17 in (430 mm) under the lavatory. Accessible counters must have clear knee space at least 17 in deep.

2. The door to the accessible toilet stall is too small at 30 in (762 mm). All door openings should be at least 36 in (900 mm) wide.

3. The grab bar on the side of the toilet is shown as 36 in (900 mm) instead of 42 in (1060 mm) long.

4. A 5 ft (1.5 m) turning circle is not shown at the change in direction at the entry door.

5. There is no accessible clearance rectangle shown at the urinal, as required.

6. Partitions are not dimensioned.

7. The lavatory is not ADA compliant at 36 in (900 mm) above finish floor (AFF). It should be no more than 34 in (865 mm).

8. The urinal mounting height is not ADA compliant at 18 in (450 mm) AFF. The maximum allowable height is 17 in.

9. The wet wall substrate is not water resistant.

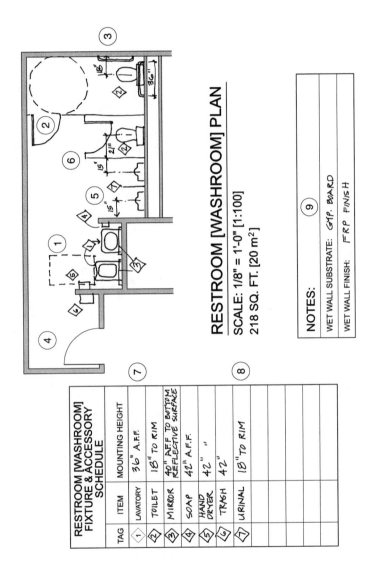

RESTROOM [WASHROOM] PLAN

SCALE: 1/8" = 1'-0" [1:100]

218 SQ. FT. [20 m²]

⑨ NOTES:

WET WALL SUBSTRATE: GYP. BOARD

WET WALL FINISH: FRP FINISH

RESTROOM [WASHROOM] FIXTURE & ACCESSORY SCHEDULE		
TAG	ITEM	MOUNTING HEIGHT
1	LAVATORY	36" A.F.F.
2	TOILET	18" TO RIM
3	MIRROR	40" A.F.F TO BOTTOM REFLECTIVE SURFACE
4	SOAP	42" A.F.F.
5	HAND DRYER	42" "
6	TRASH	42"
7	URINAL	18" TO RIM

PART C SOLUTIONS

EXERCISE 6: SYSTEMS INTEGRATION

EXERCISE 7: MILLWORK

EXERCISE 6: SYSTEMS INTEGRATION
PASSING SOLUTION

In this solution all suggestions are correctly drawn on the reflected ceiling plan. The notes in the lighting schedule and in the area for mechanical, plumbing, and electrical engineers are all communicated effectively.

NCIDQ
PRACTICUM
PRACTICE
EXAM

SYSTEMS INTEGRATION
PASSING SOLUTION

PART C

ID-6a

LIGHTING SCHEDULE

SYMBOL	DEPTH	MT. HEIGHT	DESCRIPTION
▢	7" (180 mm)		24" x 24" [600 mm x 600 mm] FLUORESCENT PARABOLIC TROFFER
▭	7" (180 mm)		24" x 48" [600 mm x 00 mm] FLUORESCENT PARABOLIC TROFFER
◐	10" (250 mm)		RECESSED WALL WASHER
○	10" (250 mm)		RECESSED DOWNLIGHT
◈	15' (380 mm)	7'-0" (2.1 m) TO BOT.	FIXED LENGTH PENDANT LIGHT FIXTURE
⊢○	4"	6'6" TO ₵	WALL SCONCE
△			TRACK LIGHTING

NOTES TO MECHANICAL, PLUMBING & ELECTRICAL ENGINEERS (FOR DESIGN INTENT INTERFACE)

NOTE NUMBER	DESCRIBE CONFLICT	DESCRIBE SOLUTION
1	light and VAV box conflict	relocate light to north
2	duct and sprinkler branch line conflict	move sprinkler branch line to south end of duct
3	files block thermostat	move thermostat
4	HVAC duct and sprinkler line conflict	relocate branch line and 3 sprinklers and connect to trunk line north of duct
5	sprinkler and light in same ceiling grid	relocate sprinkler north
6	pendant fixture too low	raise soffit to 8'-3 AFF
7	sprinkler and light in same grid	move sprinkler to south
8	track light over diffuser	move diffuser

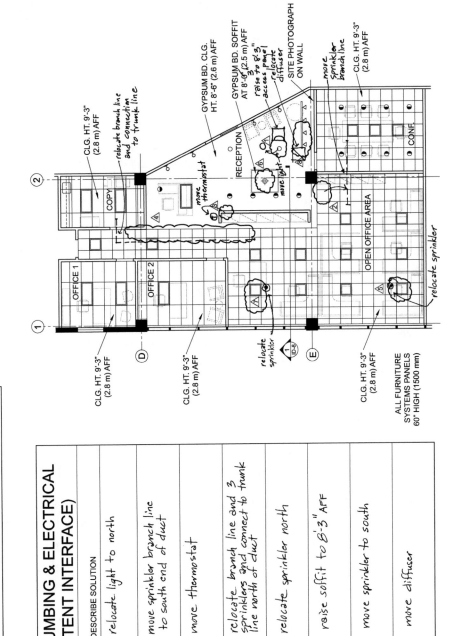

← NORTH

REFLECTED CEILING PLAN

SCALE: 1/16" = 1'-0" [1:200]

2,100 SQ. FT. [195 m²]

EXERCISE 6: SYSTEMS INTEGRATION
FAILING SOLUTION

The following errors are significant enough to contribute to the failure of this solution.

1. Wall sconces are indicated to be 6 in (150 mm) deep at a height of 60 in (1525 mm), which does not meet accessibility requirements. Items mounted on a wall between 27 in (685 mm) and 80 in (2115 mm) AFF must not protrude more than 4 in (100 mm) from the wall.

2. There is no indication of an access panel for the VAV box.

3. The solution for coordination conflict #2 indicates relocating the duct to the east to avoid the sprinkler branch line. This requires the duct to be directly connected to the VAV box, which is prohibited by the program requirements.

4. The solution for coordination conflict #3 shows the thermostat being relocated to the east side of the partition. Although this is technically possible, it would not only place the thermostat in clear view of the entry and waiting area, it would also place it in front of the luminaires, which could produce heat on the thermostat.

5. The solution for coordination conflict #4 solves the conflict between the duct and the three sprinkler heads and sprinkler branch line, but there is still interference between the duct and the connecting line to the trunk line.

6. The solution for coordination conflict #5 relocates the light to the east, but this degrades the quality of lighting and does not respect the furniture layout.

7. The solution for coordination conflict #6 is to make the pendant only 12 in (300 mm) deep. Changing the size or number of fixtures is prohibited by the program.

8. The coordination conflict #8 is resolved by moving the track light closer to the partition. However, this places the lights too close to the wall for effective illumination of the site photographs.

LIGHTING SCHEDULE

SYMBOL	DEPTH	MT. HEIGHT	DESCRIPTION
☐	7" (180 mm)		24" x 24" [600 mm x 600 mm] FLUORESCENT PARABOLIC TROFFER
☐	7" (180 mm)		24" x 48" [600 mm x 00 mm] FLUORESCENT PARABOLIC TROFFER
●	10" (250 mm)		RECESSED WALL WASHER
○	10" (250 mm)		RECESSED DOWNLIGHT
◇	15" (380 mm)	7'-0" (2.1 m) TO BOT.	FIXED LENGTH PENDANT LIGHT FIXTURE
⊢	① 6"	60" TO ₵	WALL SCONCE
◁▷			TRACK LIGHTING

NOTES TO MECHANICAL, PLUMBING & ELECTRICAL ENGINEERS (FOR DESIGN INTENT INTERFACE)

NOTE NUMBER	DESCRIBE CONFLICT	DESCRIBE SOLUTION	
△1	LIGHT UNDER VAV	MOVE LIGHT TO SOUTHWEST	
△2	SPRINKLER GOES THROUGH DUCT	MOVE DUCT AND FLEX DUCTS TO AVOID SPRINKLER LINE	③
△3	THERMOSTAT BEHIND FILES	MOVE AS SHOWN	④
△4	SPRINKLER LINE CONFLICTS W/ DUCT	RELOCATE N-S BRANCH LINE	⑤
△5	SPRINKLER/LIGHT SAME PLACE	RELOCATE LIGHT	⑥
△6	PENDANT TOO LOW	MAKE PENDANT 12" DEEP	⑦
△7	SPRINKLER/LIGHT SAME PLACE	MOVE SPRINKLER	
△8	DIFFUSER/TRACK LIGHT CONFLICT	MOVE TRACK AS SHOWN	⑧

REFLECTED CEILING PLAN

NORTH ↑

SCALE: 1/16" = 1'-0" [1:200]
2,100 SQ. FT. [195 m²]

CLG. HT. 9'-3" (2.8 m) AFF

MOVE BRANCH LINE

RELOCATE THERMOSTAT

GYPSUM BD. CLG. HT. 8'-6" (2.6 m) AFF

GYPSUM BD. SOFFIT AT 8'-0" (2.5 m) AFF

MOVE TRACK

SITE PHOTOGRAPH ON WALL

MOVE DUCT AND FLEX CONNECTIONS

CLG. HT. 9'-3" (2.8 m) AFF

COPY

RECEPTION

MOVE LIGHT

RAISE 6"

OFFICE 1

OFFICE 2

MOVE SPRINKLER

OPEN OFFICE AREA

CONF.

RELOCATE LIGHT

CLG. HT. 9'-3" (2.8 m) AFF

CLG. HT. 9'-3" (2.8 m) AFF

CLG. HT. 9'-3" (2.8 m) AFF

ALL FURNITURE SYSTEMS PANELS 60" HIGH (1500 mm)

EXERCISE 7: MILLWORK
PASSING SOLUTION

This is an excellent solution that satisfies all project requirements, provides accessibility, and is correctly shown in graphical format.

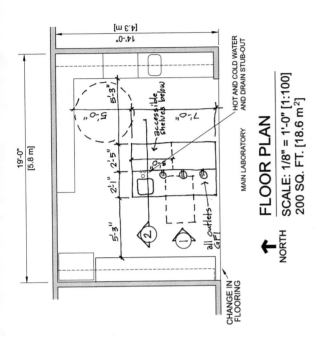

FLOOR PLAN

SCALE: 1/8" = 1'-0" [1:100]
200 SQ. FT. [18.6 m²]

NORTH

MAIN LABORATORY

HOT AND COLD WATER
AND DRAIN STUB-OUT

CHANGE IN
FLOORING

all outlets
GFI

accessible
shelves below

14'-0"
[4.3 m]

19'-0"
[5.8 m]

5'-3"

7'-0"

5'-0"

2'-1" 2'-5"

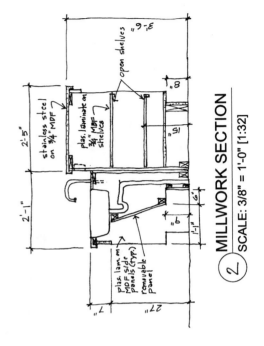

MILLWORK SECTION

SCALE: 3/8" = 1'-0" [1:32]

stainless steel
on 3/4" MDF

open shelves

plas. laminate on
3/4" MDF shelves

plas. lam. on
MDF side
panels (typ.)

removable
panel

3'-6"

2'-5"

2'-1"

8"

16"

6"

9"

1'-1"

7"

27"

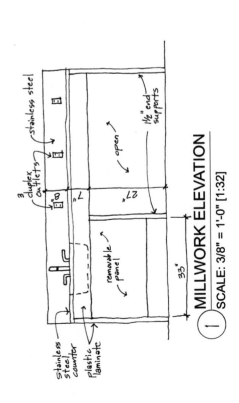

MILLWORK ELEVATION

SCALE: 3/8" = 1'-0" [1:32]

stainless steel

duplex
outlets

1½" end
supports

stainless
steel counter

plastic
laminate

removable
panel

open

33"

8"

7"

27"

EXERCISE 7: MILLWORK
FAILING SOLUTION

The following errors are significant enough to contribute to the failure of this solution.

1.   The 2 ft (600 mm) depth of the countertops shown on the floor plan drawing is shallow for a laboratory workbench. Also, it does not account for the standard 2 ft (600 mm) depth of the cabinets and other construction below. An extra inch (25 mm) or more is needed for edge overhang.

2.   There are no duplex outlets shown on the plan, section, or elevation drawings.

3.   The new island workstation is shown on the floor plan drawing with the sink directly above the plumbing stub-outs. Although technically possible, this interferes with the undercounter accessibility as shown on the section drawing.

4.   At 24 in (610 mm), the clearance of the apron is too low for accessibility. An accessible work surface must have at least 27 in (685 mm) clear knee space below. Also, other dimensions required for accessibility under the sink are not shown on the section drawing.

5.   A granite countertop, as indicated on the elevation and section drawings, is not an appropriate material for a laboratory work surface.

6.   Substrates are not indicated on the section or elevation drawings, but they are required to be by the program.

7.   The section drawing does not indicate a clear understanding of millwork construction.

8.   The work surfaces adjacent to the sink are not accessible as required by the program. As shown on the elevation, there is no clear knee space.

9.   The only protection from piping is shown as insulation around the drain, but there is no indication of protection for the hot and cold water lines on either the elevation or section drawings. In addition, the drain as shown on the drawings would interfere with accessibility.

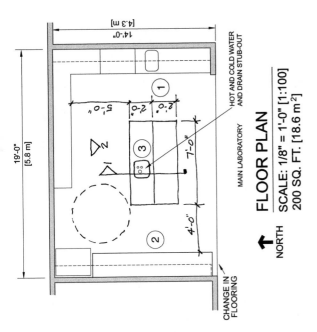

FLOOR PLAN

SCALE: 1/8" = 1'-0" [1:100]
200 SQ. FT. [18.6 m²]

NORTH

MAIN LABORATORY

HOT AND COLD WATER
AND DRAIN STUB-OUT

CHANGE IN
FLOORING

14'-0"
[4.3 m]

19'-0"
[5.8 m]

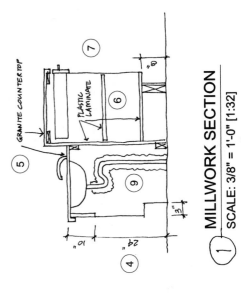

MILLWORK SECTION

SCALE: 3/8" = 1'-0" [1:32]

GRANITE COUNTERTOP

PLASTIC LAMINATE

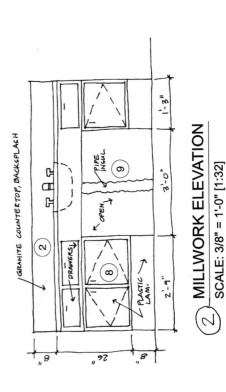

MILLWORK ELEVATION

SCALE: 3/8" = 1'-0" [1:32]

GRANITE COUNTERTOP, BACKSPLASH

PIPE INSUL.

DRAWERS

OPEN

PLASTIC LAM.